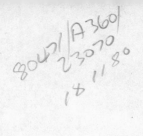

PERGAMON INTERNATIONAL LIBRARY
of Science, Technology, Engineering and Social Studies
The 1000-volume original paperback library in aid of education,
industrial training and the enjoyment of leisure
Publisher: Robert Maxwell, M.C.

THE ENGINEERING OF
MICROPROCESSOR SYSTEMS

Guidelines on System Development

THE PERGAMON TEXTBOOK
INSPECTION COPY SERVICE

An inspection copy of any book published in the Pergamon International Library will
gladly be sent to academic staff without obligation for their consideration for course adoption
or recommendation. Copies may be retained for a period of 60 days from receipt and returned
if not suitable. When a particular title is adopted or recommended for adoption for class use
and the recommendation results in a sale of 12 or more copies, the inspection copy may be
retained with our compliments. The Publishers will be pleased to receive suggestions for
revised editions and new titles to be published in this important International Library.

Other Titles of Interest

Pergamon Related Journals

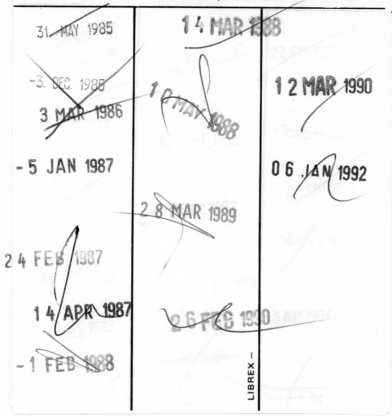

THE ENGINEERING OF MICROPROCESSOR SYSTEMS

Guidelines on System Development

The Electrical Research Association Ltd
Leatherhead, England

PERGAMON PRESS

OXFORD · NEW YORK · TORONTO · SYDNEY · PARIS · FRANKFURT

U.K.	Pergamon Press Ltd., Headington Hill Hall, Oxford OX3 0BW, England
U.S.A.	Pergamon Press Inc., Maxwell House, Fairview Park, Elmsford, New York 10523, U.S.A.
CANADA	Pergamon of Canada, Suite 104, 150 Consumers Road, Willowdale, Ontario M2J 1P9, Canada
AUSTRALIA	Pergamon Press (Aust.) Pty. Ltd., P.O. Box 544, Potts Point, N.S.W. 2011, Australia
FRANCE	Pergamon Press SARL, 24 rue des Ecoles, 75240 Paris, Cedex 05, France
FEDERAL REPUBLIC OF GERMANY	Pergamon Press GmbH, 6242 Kronberg-Taunus, Pferdstrasse 1, Federal Republic of Germany

First edition 1979

British Library Cataloguing in Publication Data

Nabavi, C D
The engineering of microprocessor systems. -
(Pergamon international library).
1. Microprocessors 2. Industrial equipment
I. Title II. Stafford, R W
621.3819'58'35   TK7895.M5   79-40952
ISBN 0-08-025435-7 Hard cover
ISBN 0-08-025434-9 Flexi cover

In order to make this volume available as economically and as rapidly as possible the typescript has been reproduced in its original form. This method has its typographical limitations but it is hoped that they in no way distract the reader.

Printed and bound in Great Britain by
William Clowes (Beccles) Limited, Beccles and London

CONTENTS

INTRODUCTION

PROJECT 0251

This volume is part of Project 0251 undertaken by The Electrical
Research Association. This first part of the Project results have
been made available by the Department of Industry under the Microprocessor Application Project (MAP).

This document provides economical and technical guidance for use
when incorporating microprocessors in products or production
processes and assesses the alternatives that are available.

Project 0251 in total consists of six volumes which are all described
in the Summary Index overleaf.*

If you require further information about Project 0251 or about ERA's
activities in general please contact,

The Electrical Research Association,
Cleeve Road, Leatherhead, Surrey, KT22 7SA, England

Telephone: Leatherhead 74151, Telex 264045.

* Only Volume 1 is available from Pergamon Press

PROJECT 0251 - SUMMARY INDEX

Volume 1 Guidelines on system development

The various steps to be taken in assessing and implementing a microprocessor based development are outlined with comments and recommendations on the available options. The report concludes with material based upon the results of a survey among users having in-house experience of specific system development. This volume is primarily aimed at management who are concerned with assessing, implementing and guiding development projects.

Volume 2 A review of development aids

A summary is given of significant software and hardware development aids currently available on the UK market. These are classified into groups and the information presented in the form of standard data sheets for ease of reference and comparison. The report is designed as a reference book on the specification and availability of particular development aids as a guide to the preliminary identification of suitable suppliers and equipment.

Volumes 3 and 4 Laboratory evaluation reports

These volumes contain the results of individual ERA laboratory tests on selected microprocessor development systems, hardware development aids and software. They are designed to provide the development engineer with a factual report of the performance, ease of use and suitability of each product.

Volume 5 Comparative assessments and glossary

Comparative data on the development systems and products tested in the laboratory is presented in this volume together with a glossary.

Volume 6 Interference and input-output

This volume deals with the effects of interference on microprocessor systems and provides guidelines on ways to minimise such effects. Input-output techniques and devices are discussed and guidelines are given on ways of connecting microprocessor systems to other devices.

VOLUME 1 GUIDELINES ON SYSTEM DEVELOPMENT

PREFACE

While attention has been focussed for some years upon the availability
and performance of microprocessors, little attention has been given
until recently to the problems of the engineer responsible for building
microprocessors into new systems and products. Early pioneers virtually
had a chip and a data sheet and took it from there. Fortunately, things
have improved since then and a range of hardware and development aids is
now available which can make life easier - but, even so, comparative
data on these is hard to find. In addition, the importance of certain
features, especially in support software, is often overlooked by the
first time user until he has gained experience the hard way.

Project O251 'The Engineering of Microprocessor Systems' was launched
by ERA to give managers and development engineers advice and comment on
the development process and the hardware and software needed to support
this. These were two basic objectives:-

- To reduce the risks of development through guidance
  on the resourcing and planning of projects.

- To improve the selection and use of hardware and
  software development aids through the provision of
  comparative data on their facilities and performance.

The programme of work, was carried out by ERA's Microprocessor Design
and Development Group in four individual phases, with consultancy
support available within a fifth phase to tackle specific client
problems. The phases were:-

Phase 1 - a review of special problems associated with micro-
            processor based systems and preparation of guide-
            lines on system development.

Phase 2 - a review and a detailed laboratory evaluation of
            microcomputer development system hardware.

Phase 3 - a review and a detailed laboratory evaluation
            of support software.

Phase 4 - overall conclusions and comparative assessment
            of systems subjected to laboratory evaluation.

Phase 5 - confidential consultancy for individual clients.

The results of Phase 1 of the project are contained in this first volume
which is aimed primarily at the manager or other users who have the
responsibility for microprocessor system developments, but who may lack
direct experience in this field. The approach has therefore been to
present an overview of the technology of microprocessors themselves, of
the development process and, of the range of development aids which will
be covered in greater depth in later volumes. In addition, we have
included wherever possible specific recommendations, facts or guidelines
on the choices to be made or procedures to be adopted. In certain areas there
is an overlap with information in ERA report 77-1 'Microprocessors -
their development and application' and readers looking for general
details on microprocessors are recommended to read this report.

It may well be that much of this volume is aimed at 'teaching your grand-
mother to suck eggs', but we make no apology for this. Indeed, it is
very clear from the survey of users carried out that gaining experience
has been and still is a major motivation behind many development projects.
It is also clear from discussions with manufacturers and distributors that
lack of basic knowledge and experience is a major factor inhibiting the
adoption of microprocessors for many other applications. For this reason,
we have included rather more detail then originally intended upon the
relative merits of different development aids.

This volume is therefore intended to provide a decision framework and
background material for management considering such developments for the
first time, so that the special problems and key aspects of a microprocessor
based development can be identified from the start.

SECTION 1

A GUIDE TO THE JARGON

1.0 A GUIDE TO THE JARGON

Throughout this report it has been necessary to use a number of terms
and acronyms which are well understood by those within the microprocessor
field. However, to some these words will be jargon and we are therefore
opening this volume with a brief explanation of the most commonly used
terms, even though these will normally be explained in the text the first
time they occur.

The first group of words we should be clear about are microprocessor,
microcomputer and minicomputer.

The second halves of these words, namely processor and computer indicate
an essential difference: The word processor refers to the central processing part of the system only, whereas the term computer implies a complete
system.   A microprocessor is the central processing part of a computer
realised on one or more purpose designed large scale integration (LSI)
circuits, as opposed to any other type of processor, made from general
purpose logic circuits.   A microcomputer contains a microprocessor plus
additional circuitry needed to complete the system. This additional
circuitry includes memory, input and output circuits, a clock generator
and maybe other related items.

A minicomputer on the other hand, although functionally equivalent to a
microcomputer is not based on a microprocessor, but is built from general
purpose logic elements. Its design is not constrained by what can be
integrated onto sub-miniature microprocessor circuits and therefore it is
generally more powerful. Minicomputers have been in existence much
longer than microcomputers, since less complex parts are required to make
them. Obviously, as technology is improving and microprocessors are getting
better, the difference between them is narrowing.   The essential difference
between microcomputers and minicomputers, as far as the user is concerned,
however, is due to their different origins.   Minicomputers are designed
and manufactured by minicomputer manufacturers who generally have extensive
software experience and can offer good support on their machines, whilst
microcomputers are designed and manufactured by semiconductor manufacturers
who do not have the same experience.   The consequences of this are
expanded upon in Section 3.

The memory of a microcomputer is used for storing the program and the data. There are two basic types of memory, namely read/write memory whose contents can be altered by writing new information into it and read only memory (ROM) whose contents are fixed. Read/write memory is usually exclusively referred to as random access memory (RAM) for historical reasons, although strictly speaking most modern read only memories can also be accessed in a random order and therefore qualify for such a description.

The essential difference as far as the user is concerned is that ROM retains the information in it even without power, even if a program error or other fault causes the system to try and overwrite the contents of the ROM. It is therefore used mainly for storing fixed programs and constants.

RAM on the other hand is referred to as volatile, i.e., it loses or forgets the information stored if the power to it is interrupted. This is the price which has to be paid if the ability to alter the information is required. RAM, therefore, is used to store variable information such as data and programs which alter. Recently, technology has advanced to the stage where non-volatile RAM's can be made. These do not lose their information when the power to them is interrupted. They are however much more expensive and do not provide such a high information density as the well established volatile RAM's.

ROM's, which are non-volatile, need to have the information loaded into them somehow before they can be used. This can either be done during the manufacturing process, they are then referred to as mask-programmed ROM's, or by the user.   In the latter case they are referred to as programmable ROM's (PROM's).   Programming is done either by burning the required information pattern into them with high voltage pulses (the fusible link type PROM's) or by storing minute charges on them. The latter are erasable through exposure to ultra-violet light and are referred to as EPROM's (erasable PROM's). After erasure a new information pattern can be pro-grammed into them; thus they lie half way between ROM's and RAM's.

Technology is now reaching the point where electrically alterable PROM's (EAPROM's) are becoming feasible.   The essential difference between these and non-volatile RAM's is that whereas the information in a RAM can be selectively altered, the information in an EAPROM can only be altered by erasing the complete contents and reloading it.

Throughout this report, extensive use has been made of the terms integrated circuit (I.C.) and chip . These terms are usually, but not always, interchangeable. A chip refers to a single piece of silicon onto which a complex circuit containing maybe thousands of transistors is etched. Usually such a chip is then packaged into a plastic or ceramic shell with the interconnections in the form of pins at the side. It is then an integrated circuit. It is also possible, but far less common, to package more than one chip into an integrated circuit.

Another term which occurs frequently is the word bit, which is derived from the words binary-digit. A bit is a single digit in the binary counting system (see below) and can have the values zero or one only. (Compare a decimal digit which can have one of ten values, namely 0 to 9). A bit is therefore the smallest unit of information. A group of eight bits is referred to as a byte. (On some older computers a byte was 6 bits wide, but this definition is no longer used). Half a byte, i.e., 4. bits, is sometimes referred to as a nibble. Although this definition presumably started as a joke, it is now becoming increasingly well established. A word is also a group of bits, but the number of bits in a word varies from computer to computer. It is usually equal to the number of bits which the computer will handle at one time. Thus a 16 bit microcomputer will have a word of 16 bits or two bytes and so on. Confusion sometimes arises here since some computers handle different numbers of bits at different times.

All commercially available microprocessors use binary arithmetic. Here numbers are represented as sums of powers of 2. For example, the binary number 1101 is equivalent to $\underline{1} \times 2^3 + \underline{1} \times 2^2 + \underline{0} \times 2^1 + \underline{1} \times 2^0$ or 13 in the more familiar decimal system. Since binary numbers tend to require large numbers of bits to represent even modestly large figures, other counting systems are often used. Ideally one would use the decimal system since this is in everyday use, but conversion between binary and decimal requires a considerable amount of mental arithmetic. Often octal is used. This is based on the radix 8 and uses the digits 0 to 7 only. Conversion between binary and octal can be performed by simply separating the binary digits (bits) into groups of three and converting each group separately. For example, the binary 100010101111 can be grouped as 100 010 101 111 which gives 4257 in octal. Since 8 bit words, i.e., bytes do not split easily into groups of 3 bits, the hexadecimal system is also often used. This is based on the radix 16 and requires 16 different digits.

Unfortunately, there are only 10 digits in normal everyday numbers, namely 0 to 9, therefore 6 more need to be invented. Usually the letters A to F are used, but sometimes Greek letters are seen. The hexadecimal digits are therefore 0, 1, 2, 3, 4, 5, 6, 7, 8, 9, A, B, C, D, E and F. To convert from binary to hexadecimal the bits are separated into groups of 4 and converted separately. For example, binary 100010101111 can be grouped as 1000 1010 1111 which gives 8AF in hexadecimal. Thus binary 100010101111 = octal 4257 = hexadecimal 8AF = decimal 2223.

Programming languages fall into two groups, namely low level or <u>assembly languages</u> and <u>high level languages</u>. In each case, the broad objective is to provide an easy means to program the microcomputer. Microcomputers themselves, of course, work by decoding rather arbitrary looking patterns of bits, the patterns being so arbitrary that programming with them directly is very error prone and tedious. It is however possible to program in binary or, as is slightly better, in octal or hexadecimal and such an activity is referred to as programming in <u>machine code</u>. An assembly language provides the user with easily memorisable mnemonic equivalents to each machine code instruction and is therefore easier to use (see Section 6), and a high level language provides a much more friendly structure and programming environment which makes programming much faster and easier. Although one assembly statement is generally equivalent to one machine code instruction, one high level statement might result in several machine code instructions. In each case the original <u>source</u> program as it is called, has to be translated into an <u>object</u> program in machine code. For this job an <u>assembler</u> or a <u>compiler</u> is needed. These are both programs which translate automatically from assembly or high level languages respectively into machine code. A fuller description of these processes is contained in Section 6 of the report.

Assemblers and compilers and other such aids need themselves to run on a computer. Such a computer is referred to as a <u>development system</u>. It is the broad objective of this project to report in detail on the availability and quality of such development systems and the assemblers, and compilers etc., which run on them.

SECTION 2

THE SIGNIFICANCE OF MICROPROCESSORS

FOR INDUSTRY

2.0 THE SIGNIFICANCE OF MICROPROCESSORS FOR INDUSTRY

Today the great majority of companies developing or manufacturing a microprocessor based product are doing so for the first time. Without doubt many more will join their ranks in the future, making their contribution to the rapidly growing use of this new technology.

But what special action, if any, is needed by these entrants to the field? Should they change their approach or policies to improve their chances of success with these new devices? And how great will be the effect on all functions of the company management?

Clearly the answer to these questions is dependent upon the type of industry, its traditional technical background and the type of product. None-the-less there are some factors which have a general relevance, particularly in those instances where a microprocessor forms a substantial part of the final product. Special features of developing microprocessor based systems are dealt with in later sections so that the comments which follow relate primarily to the other areas where the microprocessor will affect management.

2.1 New business opportunities

Perhaps the most significant fact about the microprocessor is that it creates new opportunities for business, by transforming the market size through cost reduction, by creating a totally new market through a combination of cost and performance benefits or by introducing substantial changes in existing product performance and cost which significantly affect the market potential.

The ability to spot and exploit these opportunities is clearly vital to the success of any company whose markets are affected or capable of being affected by the microprocessor. For the reasons given later this ability is now of greater importance to the company than with earlier technologies.

2.2 Product policy and life cycle

While the microprocessor creates opportunities it also creates a
problem in that the market life of a microprocessor based product
is substantially less than that of a conventional product. The
major causes of this are:

- rapid advances in microprocessor related technologies
  coupled with the falling cost of these components; it
  follows that only products using up to date technology
  and hardware are likely to be price competitive in the
  market place.

- the relative ease of reconfiguring a system through the
  use of standard modules.

- the flexibility provided by software for upgrading a
  functional specification.

- increased acceptance, or even demand, by customers of
  intelligent products.

A shortened life cycle requires in turn more accurate forecasting
and interpretation of market needs and opportunities, and a multi-
disciplinary approach to the specification and development of new
products in which there is a very close interaction between the
work of marketing, sales promotion, engineering and production.

Good modular design of hardware and software can in effect extend
the life cycle, as the inherent flexibility of a microcomputer
system can be used to provide for gradual enhancement or enable
a standard range of hardware and software modules to be used in
various combinations for a range of products. This is of course
a standard approach in other technologies but does carry with it
a potential cost penalty at the lower end of the price and
performance spectrum.

Introduction of a microprocessor usually offers the opportunity
of going 'up market'. In many cases this will be a necessary and

desirable action, technically and commercially. However, it does
carry with it the risk that the company will drift into the computer systems business without realising the full implications in
terms of high financial risk, absorption of technical effort and
need for a new breed of systems/software engineer. It is essential
to draw a clear definition of the business being sought to avoid
the sales force bringing in a demand for one off special systems
which the company is neither willing nor able to supply.

Patent protection of a product whose originality is contained within
software may well be difficult since this area is complex and un-
certain. Moreover, the shortened time over which protection will be
required makes it of less relevance.

2.3 Financial planning and control

The financial effects of using microprocessors are not easy to
quantify since they will depend to a great extent upon the significance of the microprocessor in the product cost. Microprocessors
do however introduce some special problems.

Firstly they mean a reduction in added value. Functionally larger
chips mean less connections, less boards, steelwork etc. etc. For
some industries this has already been a traumatic experience as
production has had to convert from electro-mechanical to electronic
products. The replacement of punched card machines by computers and
the introduction of solid state cash registers are two examples.
In this situation financial planning and product planning must be
closely linked to foresee the effect of change and take action
accordingly.

Secondly the trend in most semiconductor prices, especially the
recently released LSI ones, is still downwards. Market growth or
rather, sales growth, is therefore necessary just to stand still in
terms of turnover, assuming a reasonably competitive market.

These two factors create considerable pressure to increase or
maintain prices by the provision of additional performance or
operational features which can be satisfied through extra software.

In other words, added value is obtained by increasing the development expenditure, since the production cost of such software is nominal apart from the possible need for extra memory.

Thirdly the development costs are more difficult to estimate accurately due, in particular, to the introduction of software. Staff performance in software development is notoriously more variable than in other areas of development and, in addition, the control of the implementation phase is also difficult, except on the smallest projects. There is therefore a new risk factor which needs to be realistically assessed when approving a development programme.

2.4 Technical management

Using a microprocessor, with the opportunities and problems mentioned, places a greater responsibility on technical management to spot the opportunities for innovations and, having agreed on a development programme, to get it right first time. The manager needs to be fully aware of the difficulties in planning and controlling a microprocessor system development project and to have identified the strengths and weaknesses of his technical staff in this field.

The need for integration of hardware and software expertise is vital and with more standardised facilities available in both areas, development staff now require expertise at the system and sub-system level rather than at the detailed level of the past. Close inter-action with marketing staff is essential and the good design engineer will now make a greater contribution to the commercial success of the product.

Recruiting and training suitably experienced staff is a big problem as such staff are in short supply. For this reason, many of the larger companies, or those with a clear and committed policy, have launched pilot projects largely as a means of gaining experience.

2.5 Summary

The flexibility and adaptability of microprocessor systems result in a shorter market life in which management control is critical. The lack of experience in this field at both management and engineering

levels makes microprocessor projects somewhat unpredictable, but
this is counteracted by the resultant product flexibility and low
production costs.   The intelligent nature of many products requires
a much closer cooperation between hardware, software and marketing
staff.   New expertise is required and training becomes much more
important than before.   The lower added value and increased
number of smaller production runs place a greater burden on management.
The nett result will probably be that firms will either be very
successful, or will abandon the market altogether.   There is no room
for mediocrity.

SECTION 3

CHOOSING THE RIGHT TECHNOLOGY

3.O <u>CHOOSING THE RIGHT TECHNOLOGY</u>

An electronic designer, faced with the problem of engineering a system today, is confronted with a wide choice of implementation methods. Even problems which are basically analogue in nature can now be solved effectively using digital or computer based techniques.

Analogue design techniques are well established and understood and therefore need little comment here. Suffice it to say that modern analogue components are in general easy to use and the designer can implement a system using highly stable operational amplifiers and other module-like integrated circuits such as multiplexers. The main problems, however, are still in the areas of noise, capacitive cross coupling and calibration. These areas do not usually cause problems in digital implementations, though of course there are others. It is now becoming economical to process analogue signals digitally by digitising the signal, carrying out the required function digitally and then converting back with a digital to analogue convertor. Applications of this tech- nique include digital speech transmission using pulse code modulation and digital processing of seismic waveforms.

Digital techniques fall into two main groups, namely serial and parallel. Computer implementations are essentially serial in that they implement the various parts of the total process sequentially. The concept of a parallel processor refers to the fact that a processor deals with a group of bits, i.e., a word at once or in parallel, rather than sequentially. This means that all implementations based on computer techniques are slower than possible non-computer implementations discussed later.

The user of microprocessors needs at least a familiarity with the major characteristics of different semiconductor technologies if he is to be able to select suitable devices to meet his system requirements. He also needs to understand when to use the various implementation techniques, such as hard wired logic, custom LSI and minicomputers etc., in preference to microprocessors. These two topics are discussed in this section and the advantages and disadvantages of the different technologies and tech- niques are pointed out.

3.1 Modern semiconductor technology

The most important characteristics of the major semiconductor families are described below. The numerous variations of the major classifications are not covered, and the reader is referred to ERA's Report 77-1 'Microprocessors - their development and application' for more detailed information should he require it.

These major technologies are shown in Fig.3.1-1. The first subdivision is between bipolar and metal oxide semiconductor (MOS), which are derived from normal transistors and field effect transistors respectively. As far as the user is concerned, the most important distinctions between the two lie in the fact that bipolar circuits are basically low impedance devices which consume more power, cannot be packed so densely onto a chip and are faster, whereas MOS circuits are high impedance devices which consume less power, are suitable for high density packing and are not so fast. Although this is somewhat of an oversimplification, it will often suffice. The subdivisions of these two basic technologies obviously contain their own spread of characteristics, which lead to a blurring of the differences outlined above. Each of these will now be briefly discussed in turn.

3.1.1 Transistor-transistor-logic (TTL)

Transistor-transistor-logic (TTL), the best known bipolar logic family, is extremely popular for general purpose logic.

A wide range of simple to medium complexity circuits are available such as NAND gates, registers, decoders, arithmetic units etc. It is fairly robust, easy to design with and multiply sourced (reference any 74 Series TTL catalogue). There are several variations of standard TTL, the original ones being low power and high power TTL.

Low power TTL is suitable for lower speed systems and high power TTL for higher speed circuits. These two variations are not as popular as standard TTL.

Another important variation is Schottky TTL. This gives a greatly improved speed without increased power consumption. Nowadays the Schottky process is usually applied to low power TTL which gives a family with the speed of standard TTL, with a saving of 80% in power consumption. Low power Schottky TTL is fast becoming the most popular form of TTL, instead of

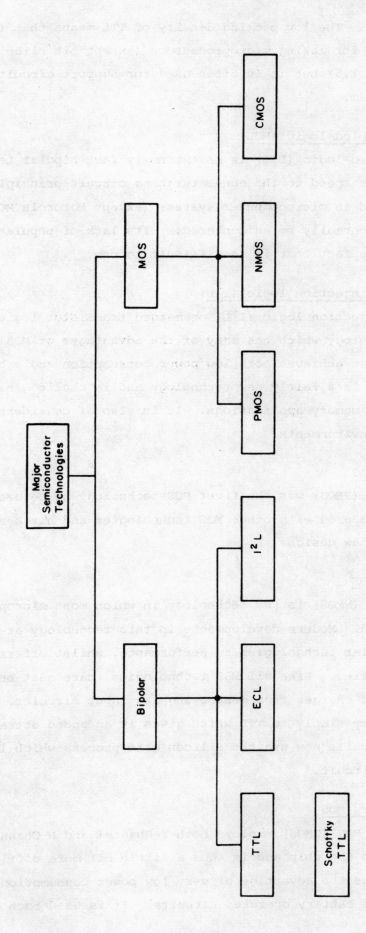

FIG. 3·1—1   MAJOR SEMICONDUCTOR TECHNOLOGIES

standard TTL.   The low packing density of TTL means that it is not normally used for making microprocessors (except bit slice microprocessors - see Section 4.1.5) but it is often used for support circuits in a micro-computer system.

3.1.2 Emitter-coupled-logic (ECL)

Emitter-coupled-logic (ECL) is an extremely fast bipolar technology which owes its speed to the non-saturating circuit principles employed. It is rarely used in microcomputer systems (except Motorola MC10800 series) and will not normally be encountered.   Its lack of popularity probably stems from the fact that it is difficult to use.

3.1.3 Integrated injection logic (I^2L)

Integrated injection logic (I^2L) or merged transistor logic (MTL) is a bipolar technology which has many of the advantages of MOS circuits. It is fast and yet achieves both low power consumption and a high packing density.   It is a fairly new technology and is challenging MOS for micro-processor and memory applications. It is also of considerable interest in military environments.

3.1.4 P-Channel MOS

P-Channel MOS (PMOS) was the first MOS technology to be used extensively. It is slow compared with other MOS technologies and has been replaced by NMOS in most new designs.

3.1.5 N-Channel MOS

N-Channel MOS (NMOS) is the technology in which most microprocessors are now fabricated. Modern developments in this technology are making it approach bipolar technologies in performance, whilst offering very high circuit densities. Like all MOS technologies, care must be taken to prevent static charges from destroying its input circuits. NMOS can be interfaced very simply to TTL which gives it an added attraction over PMOS. Most NMOS circuits now use the silicon gate process which leads to a fairly fast circuit.

3.1.6 Complementary MOS

Complementary MOS (CMOS) employs both P-Channel and N-Channel field effect transistors on the chip and is thus a little bit more difficult to make. However, it has the advantage of very low power consumption, and is there-fore ideal for battery operated circuits. It is used both as a standard logic family in competition to TTL and as a microprocessor technology. Unlike other technologies, CMOS does not require a highly stabilised power supply. When the correct supply voltage is used, it can be interfaced to TTL fairly easily.

3.2 Modern system implementation techniques

Microprocessors do not of course always provide the best way to implement a particular system and it is therefore worth considering other possibilities. Figure 3.2-1 shows the basic family of techniques that can be used. As can be seen the digital area with which we are concerned splits into two distinct sections, one covering techniques where the function is fixed by a program, e.g., microprocessors, the other covering techniques where the function is fixed by the physical layout or interconnection of devices. This category of course covers custom LSI and conventional hard wired logic systems.

In considering these possibilities it is essential that the criteria by which they will be judged are clear, so that the best implementation technique for the particular situation is recognised. And, while the best may often be the cheapest, it could equally be that the most flexible, quickest to design or whatever is to be preferred. The comments which follow are therefore designed to discuss the relative merits of the major competitors to a microprocessor solution and to give general guidelines on the factors which will influence the decision. In this way, the designer can evaluate the relative merits of each one in his own particular circumstances.

3.2.1 Microprocessors and microcomputers

As we have already seen, a microprocessor is the central processing part of a computer realised on one or more purposed-designed LSI chips. A microcomputer on the other hand is a fully working computer based upon a microprocessor, containing all the necessary additions to make a fully working system.

The design of a microprocessor based system can be broken down into two parts, namely the hardware and software. The design of hardware is becoming very straightforward, since modern microprocessors and their associated peripheral and memory components can be virtually plugged together without the need for detailed logic design which was previously the norm. There is still a choice, however, to be made between hardware

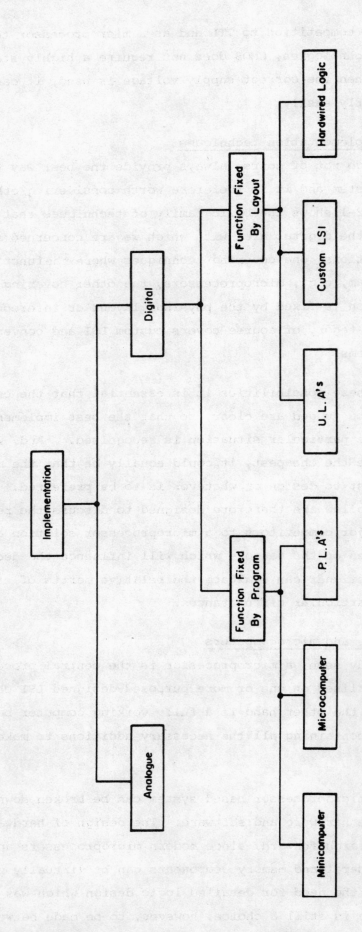

FIG. 3·2—1 MODERN IMPLEMENTATION TECHNIQUES.

designed specifically for the particular application and a general
purpose microcomputer card which requires the minimum of special logic.
This choice will be based upon the anticipated production volumes and the
relative cost and risk of implementing a system in either form.

Typical costs of such a general purpose card would be between £200 and
£800 depending upon the microprocessor type and facilities provided on
the card. If we assume that the more complex board would take an
engineer two months to design and test and assume a salary of £5000 x 2.4
to allow for overheads (this is an average taken from ERA's survey of
users, but readers can apply their own figures) plus £500 for board layout
+ assembly, then the development cost will be £2500. The recurring costs,
consisting of components and assembly are likely to come to about £300 for
the more complex boards and about half that for the simpler boards. In
this cost region therefore it is worth designing one's own boards for
quantities greater than about 5 off. In practice the resultant delay to
the project, associated risk and drain on valuable management and engineering resources is likely to increase this breakeven point to around 10 off.
The actual quantity for a specific case must however take into consideration the fact that a purpose built board will usually contain less components than a general purpose board. It is therefore necessary to
evaluate each specific situation carefully.

By contrast with the hardware, software design is likely to be a problem
for many organisations and the effort required to implement a program is
often grossly underestimated. Standard, proven hardware can therefore
be an additional advantage when time and development cost are critical.
As microprocessor manufacturers improve the range of components and
boards available, the advantage of using these standard facilities against
a purpose built design will become greater, at least in the initial stages
of a new product development.

In considering the overall cost of using a microprocessor or microcomputer
the survey mentioned earlier disclosed an average labour cost of £34,000
(34 man months). While this may to some seem a high figure, it should be
remembered that it includes all effort associated with taking the initial
concept through to preproduction. On this basis, in ERA's experience, it
is not untypical of the medium range project which might, for example,
be the development of a new microprocessor based instrument. In addition,

the breakdown of effort into the separate tasks on a percentage basis provides a convenient method of comparison with estimates for a specific case. However, use of standard hardware in the form of a single board microprocessor or readymade input/output circuits will clearly alter the ratio of hardware to software effort.

As will be seen later, the decision upon whether to use a microprocessor is influenced very considerably by factors other than cost, but neverthe-less, the true development cost is an important factor.

3.2.2 Minicomputers

Often the best way to implement a system is with a minicomputer. Although a minicomputer costs considerably more than a microcomputer, minicomputers have several advantages. The first is that a minicomputer is a fully engineered system which requires no further hardware design. Interfacing is usually straightforward and therefore the system can become functional quickly and with little effort. The second advantage is that the manu-facturer's support is traditionally much better and, if an established supplier is used, there is likely to be a wide range of software packages available. These points are very important for small production quanti-ties for which the development costs are likely to be a significant part of the total cost.

Minicomputers usually cost between £4000 and £30000 depending on the type and configuration, with a typical figure for a small system of between £6000 and £10000. It is very difficult to quantify the advantages gained by the increased support traditionally obtainable from minicomputer suppliers. According to the results of the ERA survey, a typical micro-processor project costs £40000, of which the labour content is £34000. Users generally agreed that the use of a minicomputer would reduce these development costs by 20%, but would increase the production costs by 50%. (There was a high degree of correlation in the individual assessments of these values.)   These figures indicate that use of a minicomputer would be economic for quantities of up to three to four units, a figure which is considerably lower than expected. It must be noted though that in this particular case, this figure is very sensitive to minor alterations in the assumptions on which the results are based, such as the relative difference in development and production costs and the cost of the final product. It is therefore essential to evaluate these calculations against data applicable to the particular situation.

3.2.3 Hard wired logic

The term hard wired logic refers to the traditional method of implementing a digital function using 'and' gates and flip-flops etc. The most common form of this is standard TTL (transistor transistor logic). This is now being superseded by low power Schottky TTL. Earlier forms of logic such as RTL (resistor transistor logic) and DTL (diode transistor logic) are no longer used in new designs, except for discrete versions of DTL which is compatible with TTL and is often used for interfacing to higher power circuits such as lamp drivers.

When higher integration densities or lower power consumption is required, one of the many forms of MOS logic (metal oxide semiconductor) is usually used. Most microprocessors and many of their peripherals are implemented in this technology.

Since the various parts of the total function can be implemented as separate sub-units which can all work simultaneously, i.e., a parallel realisation, hard wired logic is potentially very fast. It is anticipated that hard wired logic will to a large extent be superseded by microprocessor and custom LSI implementations, which use less power and occupy less space. Hard wired logic, however, cannot be beaten when high speed is required. This is unlikely to change in the near future unless great improvements are made in the custom LSI area.

The general consensus of opinion in the ERA survey was that a hard wired logic system would cost 50% more to develop than its microprocessor based equivalent and two and a half times as much to produce. These figures agree approximately with ERA's own experience, at least in medium complexity systems. This means that unless the task requires the high speed attainable only with hard wired logic, then microprocessors are always more attractive, regardless of quantity and are likely to become increasingly so.

3.2.4 Custom LSI

Custom LSI is similar to hard wired logic with the essential difference that the interconnections between the various logic elements are done by the semiconductor manufacturer at chip level. In other words, the design is performed in much the same way as conventional hard wired logic and then this design is implemented on a single integrated circuit. Obviously the

logic elements are different and the design constraints very different.
The design process requires a much more basic knowledge of circuit design
and of course a deep understanding of semiconductor technology. Unlike
hard wired logic, it is not possible to make minor alterations to the
circuit at breadboard level; it either works first time or it does not.
The design of custom LSI must therefore be done very carefully using
highly skilled engineers and is therefore very costly, but once done, it
leads to very low unit costs. It is therefore ideal for very high volume
applications.   The amount of logic that can be implemented on a single
chip is of course limited and so custom LSI is not suitable for very complex functions.

The present capacity of most custom LSI manufacturers is limited by the
available design capacity in this field, rather than by the processing
capability of their plants. This means that they tend only to accept
contracts involving design work if this is to be followed by large volume
production. In other words, the volume at which it becomes economical
to use custom LSI is artificially high because of the marketing policies
of the semiconductor manufacturers.

Generally speaking, quantities in the region of 100,000 to 250,000 have
to be guaranteed before the manufacturers become interested and will
allocate design effort to the project. However, this is not a fixed
quantity range and a figure of 15,000 per year was given by one manufacturer recently who had spare design effort at the time. Prices for a
simple logic circuit in quantities where the development costs are
negligible (e.g. 100,000) can be as low as £2 per chip. This compares
very favourably with prices of single chip microcomputers. Since the
breakeven point is determined more by political considerations than by
economic ones, there is little point trying to calculate it with any
accuracy. If quantities are likely to be over, say, 40,000 within a
period of two to three years, it is at least worth approaching the custom
LSI manufacturer to try to extract a quotation.

If one can provide an LSI manufacturer with the masks (in other words have
the design done elsewhere) then he is much more likely to agree to supply
relatively small quantities. Although there are a few separate custom
LSI design facilities, most of them are owned by large manufacturing organisations, for which they provide a design service. This has the advantages

of keeping the proprietary designs confidential, permitting the economical
use of custom LSI for medium quantity production and maintaining independence from single custom LSI suppliers. One of the problems that such
custom LSI design establishments face is complying with the various so
called design rules used by the different manufacturers. These rules
cover things like permissible track widths and spacing etc. and vary considerably from one manufacturer to another. (For comparison, a common
design rule in printed circuit board layout is that not more than one
track be led between the pins of an integrated circuit.) The obvious way
to proceed is to try and conform with all the rules of all possible custom
LSI suppliers, but this leads to an unworkable set of rules. The best
that one can hope for is a set of rules which will cover two or three
suppliers.

3.2.5 Uncommitted logic arrays (ULA's)

The idea behind an uncommitted logic array (ULA) is similar to that of
custom LSI, in that both are tailor made integrated circuits. In custom
LSI, the circuit is designed from scratch, possibly using modules such as
flip-flops etc., whereas in a ULA design, as much of the general circuit
design as possible is carried out in a general fashion, the tailoring
being left to the last minute. A ULA consists of a matrix of components
on a single chip, but with no interconnections. To implement a specific
function, aluminium interconnections are put onto the ULA in a single
masking operation. This means that the design is relatively simple
compared with custom LSI, although it is not so flexible.

A typical ULA consists of a couple of thousand components arranged in a
matrix of about two hundred cells. Starting from a logic diagram, a ULA
would take about four months to develop and cost about £2,000. Production
costs range from £15 per chip for a high complexity circuit at 1,000
units per year to £2 per chip for a low complexity circuit at 100,000 units
per year. These prices compare very favourably with custom LSI prices;
the main difference being between 10,000 and 40,000 units per year where
ULA's are still attractive. Between 40,000 and 100,000 units per year,
either approach could be most economical, depending on the design capacity
of the manufacturer. As already explained, this is likely to affect their
willingness to cooperate and hence presumably the price. In quantities
above 100,000 custom LSI starts becoming much more attractive unless the
design time, typically one year, is too long, in which case ULA's might
still be preferred.

3.2.6 Programmable logic arrays (PLA's)

Many combinatorial logic functions can be implemented using read only memories (ROM's). To do this, the inputs are used as an address and the desired response corresponding to the inputs is stored at that address. An eight input line, twelve output line function, would require a 2^8 x 12 bit, i.e., 3072 bit memory, which is perfectly feasible as a single chip circuit. However, a sixteen input line, 12 output line requires 2^{16} x 12 bits, i.e. 786,432 bits, which is not yet feasible on a single chip. A practical requirement may very well have sixteen inputs and twelve outputs, but most of the possible input combinations are never likely to occur. It is in such areas that PLA's are most useful.

A PLA can be regarded as a ROM with most of the words missing, i.e. most address combinations give zero output (see Fig.3.2.6-1). The definition of the function of a PLA falls therefore into two parts. Firstly, the addresses or input combinations which are meaningful must be identified, and secondly the output functions at those addresses must be defined. In practice, there is considerable flexibility here, since the definition of the required input combination can and usually does incorporate don't care conditions on some of the inputs. The complete design process can be described mathematically and implemented algorithmically, possibly on a digital computer. Although the maths and theory behind the procedures is not complex, it is unfamiliar to most designers, which is possibly why PLA's are not used as much as they deserve.

When some of the outputs are fed back to the inputs via a clocked register, sequential circuits can also be implemented and complex functions realised. Such techniques will be familiar to designers of microprogrammed computers.

Field programmable logic arrays (FPLA's) are also available. These can be programmed by the user and are ideal for prototyping work and small pro- duction runs. A typical FPLA might have 16 address inputs and 8 outputs. When implemented with a ROM, 65536 bytes would be required. In an FPLA typically only 48 of these would exist. Such a PLA would be referred to as a 48 product term PLA.

Mask programmed PLA's are probably not of great interest to most designers since the competition from ULA's and custom LSI gives a higher logic density. For small quantities where neither custom LSI nor ULA's are

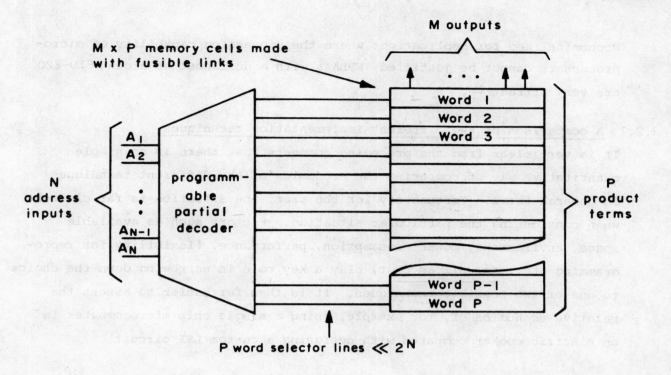

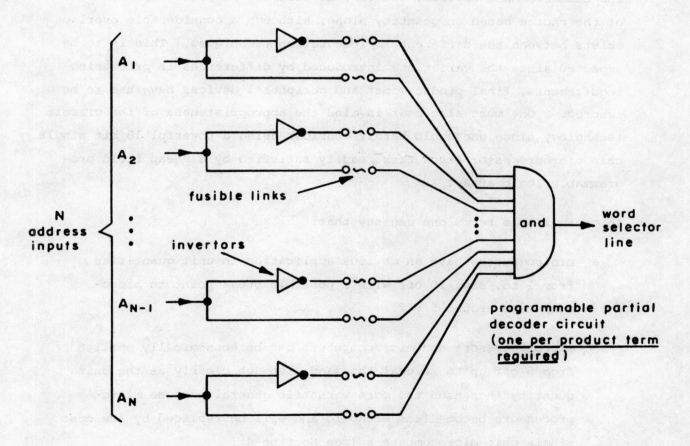

FIG. 3·2·6–1   THE IMPLEMENTATION OF A PLA.

economical and for applications where the processing capability of micro-processors cannot be justified, FPLA's with a unit cost of around £10-£20 are very attractive.

3.2.7 A comparison of the different implementation techniques

It is very clear from the preceding comments that there is no simple quantitative way of comparing the economics of the different techniques in general terms. Fortunately for the user, the situation is far clearer when considering the particular situation. Factors such as available space, environment, power consumption, performance, flexibility for repro-gramming etc., as well as cost, play a key role in narrowing down the choice to one or two possible techniques. It is then far easier to assess the relative economics of, for example, using a single chip microcomputer in an electric cooker compared with designing a custom LSI circuit.

The comments made earlier, however, do enable a simplified presentation of the choice based on quantity alone, although a considerable overlap exists between the different implementation techniques. This is to be expected since the variations introduced by differences in processing requirements, final product cost and peripheral devices have had to be ignored. One must also bear in mind the appropriateness of the circuit technology since one would hardly consider using a powerful 16 bit single chip microprocessor for a task readily satisfied by a cheap field pro-grammable logic array.

In these simple terms one can say that:

- minicomputers have an obvious application in unit quantities from 1 to, say, 10 off with a possible break point to micro-computers around 5 off.

- microprocessors and microcomputers can be economically applied from 5 off up to several thousand although clearly as the unit quantity increases the more versatile general purpose micro-processors become less economic and will be replaced by low cost single chip microcomputers (see Section 4).

- programmable logic arrays are not likely to offer attraction in their conventional form but the field programmable version (FPLA) can be economic in quantities from one off up to 2 or 3 thousand.

- uncommitted logic arrays compete with custom LSI in the region from 10,000 to 100,000 but the balance probably switches in favour of custom LSI at around 40,000 if the manufacturer is interested.

- custom LSI comes into its own around 100,000 but this is an artificial break point largely imposed by manufacturers and the availability of design effort.

SECTION 4

SELECTING THE MICROPROCESSOR

4.0 SELECTING THE MICROPROCESSOR

The choice of a microprocessor for any given application will depend
upon a number of factors which are discussed in this section. One of
these is the architecture and associated processing power. A convenient method of comparison is to divide the complete performance
spectrum into five classes of microprocessor or microcomputer and
these are described in the first part of this section.   Most applications can be satisfied from these five classes so that a first choice
of the type of microprocessor needed can then be made fairly easily.

An analysis follows of some of the major microprocessors and microcomputers, identifying their position in this performance spectrum.
The aim of this is not to provide basic information on the architecture and instruction set, for this is readily available from the manufacturers' data sheets or reports such as ERA 77-1 "Microprocessors,
their development and application", but to pinpoint some of the less
obvious aspects and characteristics of their design.

Good support from the manufacturer and his market standing are also
important factors, perhaps the most important in the majority of
situations. The quality of support software and compatible memory
and input-output circuits in particular should be a major influence on
the choice.   Evaluation of the former, of course, forms a major part
of Project O251 and will be reported on in Phase 3.   In this section
the commercial standing and market position are the main interest.

Finally, the section concludes with some general comments on the
importance of a number of other factors which will clearly be significant in any choice.

4.1 Classes of microprocessor

Traditionally, microprocessors have been classified according to their
bit lengths.   The most common bit lengths are 4, 8 and 16 bits,
although one bit and 12 bit microprocessors are also available.

Although the processing power of a microprocessor is very much influenced by its bit length, other characteristics are more likely to provide a better means of classifying them into different processing power groups and hence give a rough idea as to their suitability for different applications. The technology in which they are implemented is one example, since bipolar microprocessors are in general much faster than MOS devices, but require more integrated circuit packages to implement a microcomputer. In fact, a very useful way of classifying microprocessors is by the number of chips required to implement a microcomputer and this has been used below.

4.1.1 Single chip microcomputers

At the bottom end of the spectrum there are single chip microcomputers (See Fig.4.1.1-1) which contain the microprocessor, a small amount of RAM and ROM, a clock generator and sufficient input/output logic to make them usable for simple systems (eg. the Texas Instruments TMS 1000). Since the ROM is on the chip, such a microcomputer can only be used in a dedicated environment and the program must be loaded into the ROM in a masking operation at the time of manufacture. This technique is suitable only for fairly large production runs as the masking charges are high. Because the complete microcomputer is integrated onto a single chip, the various parts have to be kept simple. This means that such microcomputers tend to be of a low processing power compared to other devices of the same design date. It is worth noting at this point, that the integration density, ie, the number of elements that can be incorporated onto a chip is doubling approximately every two years, so generalisations like the one above should be treated with care.

A recent variation of the single chip microcomputer (eg. Intel 8748) incorporates a field programmable and erasable ROM on the chip. This is extremely useful for prototyping work and for field trials etc. and can be used for small production runs.

4.1.2 Two chip microcomputers

The next class worth considering is the two chip microcomputer (See Fig.4.1.2-1).

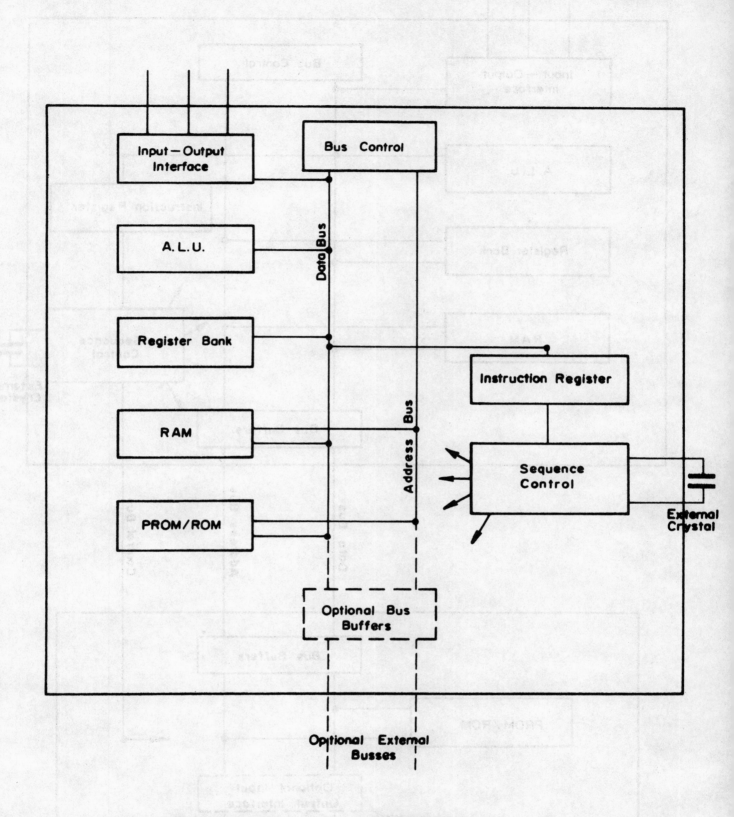

FIG. 4·1·1—1   IDEALISED   SINGLE   CHIP   MICROCOMPUTER.

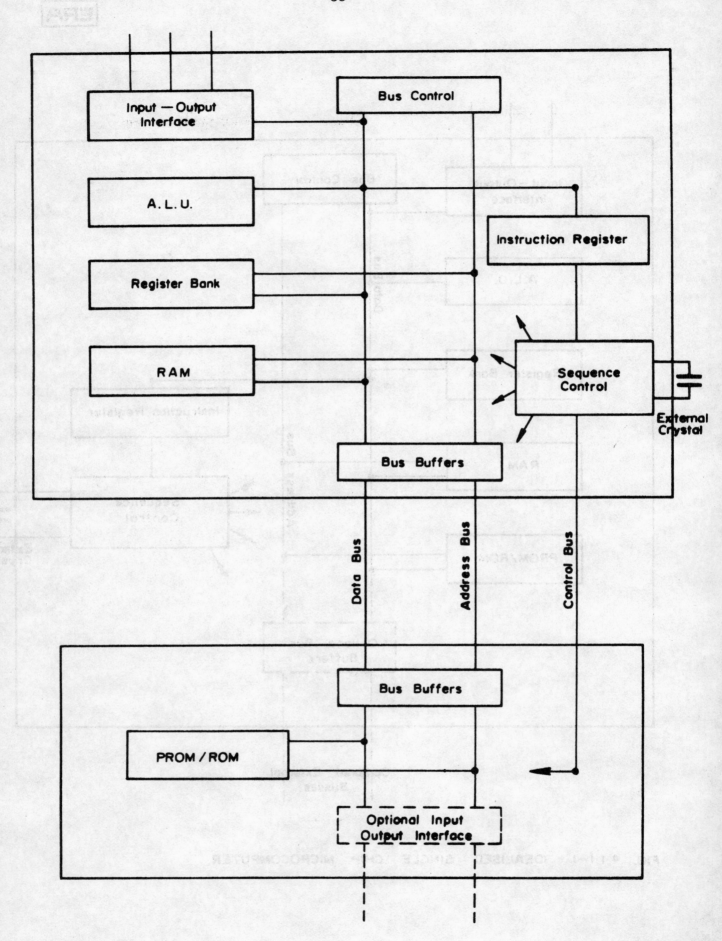

FIG. 4·1·2—1 IDEALISED TWO CHIP MICROCOMPUTER

In this class the microcomputer is, in the ideal case, partitioned such that the ROM is one chip and everything else on the other. A standard ROM can then be used, or for prototyping or development purposes, even a RAM or field programmable ROM. In practice the partitioning is not normally so clean cut which means that standard ROM's cannot be used, (eg. on the Fairchild F8). In the interests of reducing the total chip count to a minimum, the manufacturers usually partition the microcomputer such that other devices can be incorporated onto the ROM chip. There are for example ROM and RAM chips with input-output ports and with timers etc. on the chip. Although this is desirable in many ways, it does reduce the overall design freedom of the engineer designing the system.

4.1.3 Single chip microprocessors

The single chip microprocessor (See Fig. 4.1.3-1), as typified by the Intel 8080 or the Motorola 6800, is the most popular type at present. These devices can be put together in a variety of ways with other standard support chips to make various configurations which can approach the power of conventional minicomputers. The 8080 and 6800 are the two most significant members of this group and account for the major part of the total microcomputer market. They typically require ten to twenty chips for a minimum system. More modern additions to this class such as the Intel 8085 require only three chips to make a working microcomputer.

4.1.4 Single board computers

There are two main types of single board computer, namely those supplied by minicomputer manufacturers and those supplied by micro-processor manufacturers or semiconductor houses. The former, typified by the Digital Equipment Corporation LSI 11 tend to be more expensive, but are much better supported. A complete range of working support software is usually available on the minicomputer from which they evolved, and this means that systems based on them can be developed quickly and efficiently.

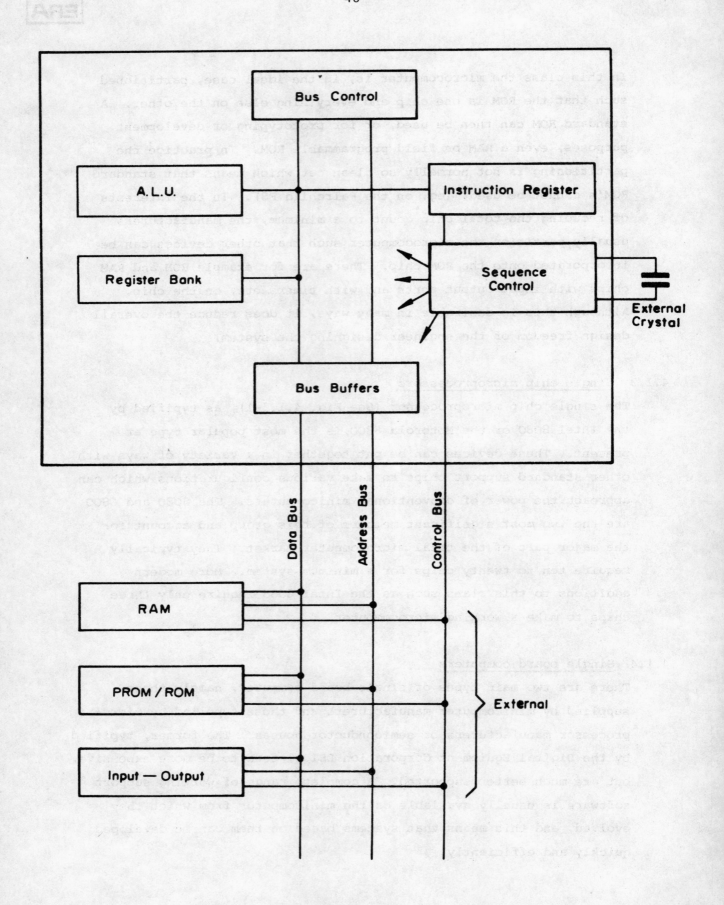

FIG. 4·1·3—1   IDEALISED   SINGLE   CHIP   MICROPROCESSOR.

The boards available from the microprocessor manufacturers, eg. the Intel SBC 80/20 are probably most useful as a means of implementing a prototype system where the production quantities will later warrant the design of a tailor made board based on the same microprocessor as that which is used on the single board computer. They also find application in areas where a design team has experience of a particular microprocessor but where the application does not warrant its own special design. Single board computers are best used in low quantity production volumes in which the design effort required to realise a tailor made system cannot be justified.

4.1.5 Microprogrammable multichip microprocessors

When the power of a single chip microprocessor is inadequate, one of the multichip sets can be used (See Fig. 4.1.5-1). In these, the microprocessor is usually partitioned onto several chips such that the arithmetic logic unit (ALU) and the registers are divided into slices, typically two or four bits wide and the control section is separated from these and placed on a separate chip.

For example, in a system based on the AMD 2900 series, which is partitioned into 4 bit slices, a 16 bit microprocessor could be built up with 4 ALU chips and one control chip. Considerably more has to be done however before such a system approaches the function of a single chip microprocessor. These chip sets are usually microprogrammable, which means that the designer must first design the microprocessor and implement the instruction set with a microprogram. This is a program which controls the operation of the microprocessor itself and is not something with which most designers come in contact.

A typical microprocessor using these techniques is likely to occupy a complete board (without memory etc.) but it offers considerable advantages in terms of speed and flexibility. The design of such microprogrammable multichip microprocessors is not something which can be recommended to the first time user. There are however ready made boards which are based on such devices and these can be recommended when very high speed is required.

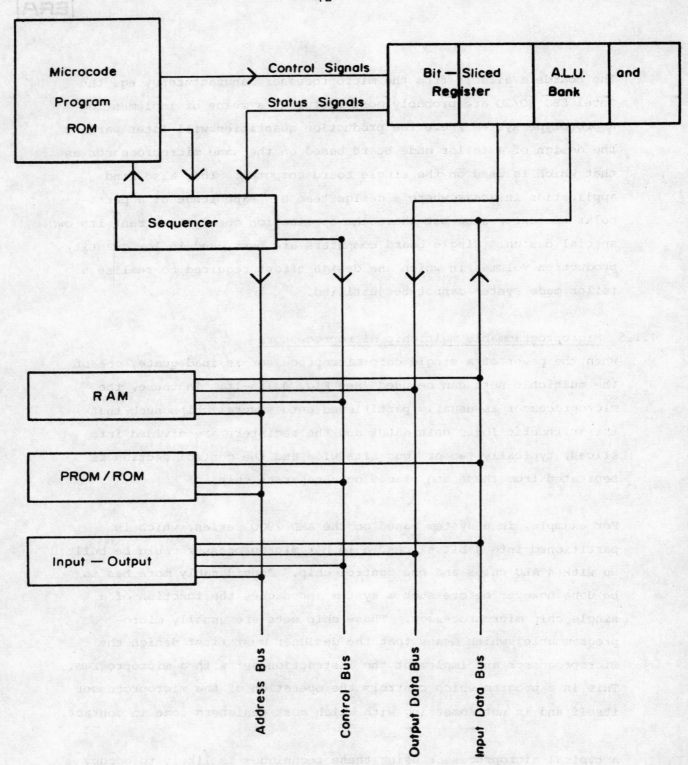

FIG. 4·1·5—I IDEALISED BIT—SLICED MICROPROGRAMMED MICROCOMPUTER

4.2 An appraisal of some major microprocessors

In order to appreciate the reasons why certain microprocessors are
better than others it is important to recognise the major constraints
within which the microprocessor designer has to work. The three
greatest constraints are firstly the number of logic elements which
can be integrated onto a single chip, secondly the number of pins
which can be accommodated on the package, and thirdly the speed of
operation of the basic gate circuits used. The permissible power
dissipation is one of the factors which limit the integration density
and speed. The achievable integration density has been doubling
every two years recently and is expected to continue to do so for
some time. Speed is also improving, partly due to new techniques
and partly because higher density integration implies lower self
capacitance and therefore higher speed.

Bearing these constraints in mind, it is easy to see that the designer
must make certain trade-offs in terms of bit length, processing speed
and architecture. As far as the architecture is concerned from the
users point of view, the design can provide a microprocessor with
many registers, many instructions, many addressing modes etc., but
not all of these.

The trend towards 16 bit microprocessors is in some ways premature,
since technology has not yet advanced to the stage where the number
of logic gates which can be integrated onto a single chip is no
longer a limiting factor. This means that, in order to achieve a
16 bit architecture, other sacrifices have to be made. This fact is
noticeable in many of the 16 bit microprocessors presently available.

4.2.1 Intel 4004 and 4040

The Intel 4004 was the first microprocessor to be made commercially
available. Although it represented a significant breakthrough at
the time of its introduction in 1972, technology has advanced so
fast that the 4004 is no longer of interest in new product design.
The 4040, which is an enhanced version of the 4004, is similarly of
little interest nowadays except for use in earlier designs. Both
processors are however, still available and are supported by a wide
range of compatible input-output and memory chips.

4.2.2 Intel 8008

The Intel 8008 is, like the 4004, a rather difficult processor to use. It requires a large number of standard logic circuits to make it work and is rather elementary in its instruction repertoire. Like the 4004, it is no longer used in new designs. Its significance is due to the fact that it paved the way for the introduction of the 8080.

4.2.3 Intel 8080

The Intel 8080 was the first relatively convenient to use single chip microprocessor. Unlike its predecessors, it contains no inherent limitations which prevent the programmer from accomplishing any particular task, given enough time. This means that, for example, subroutines can be nested to any depth, subroutine arguments are possible, all types of data and control structure are possible and all possible operations are achievable through the combination of the basic instructions. It can therefore be regarded as the first true general purpose microprocessor. To clarify this point, a few examples are required; in the 8008 it was impossible to:

- nest subroutines more than 8 levels deep
- perform computed jumps or computed subroutine calls
- use the stack for data storage
- read the program counter
- have subroutines with arguments
- have genuine relocatable code

It must be emphasised that some of the above operations are extremely tedious to perform on the 8080. They are nevertheless possible, whereas on the 8008 they were all impossible. Because of the generality of the 8080 it is very widely used, and, because it was introduced as long ago as December 1973, it has become an industry standard. Many people do not like it however, because it requires three power supply voltages, has a somewhat messy instruction set (which had to be compatible with the 8008) and its addressing facilities are not very good. It is now available from many suppliers and is extremely well supported by peripheral chips.

4.2.4 Intel 8085

The 8085 is a slightly improved version of the 8080, rather than a
new processor. The main differences are that the interfacing has
been tidied up by incorporating the clock generator on the chip,
rearranging the bus structure, slightly enhancing the interrupt
capabilities and eliminating two of the power supplies. A 50%
speed increase has also been achieved. Two new instructions are
provided to handle the new interrupts.

Viewed on its own, this does not represent very much of an improvement over the 8080, particularly in medium or large systems where
the one or two chips saved by the new architecture will not have
much affect on the overall complexity. However, when the 8085 is
used with two further specially designed circuits, a three chip
computer is possible. These circuits are multifunction chips with
memory, input-output and timers on single chips. In some senses this
represents a step backwards in the direction of the 4004 and its
associated circuits, since it departs from the generalised bus
structure to which peripherals and memory could be attached at will.
However, the 8085 can be adapted to this general bus structure by the
addition of a single latch, which makes it look similar to an 8080
with a system controller chip.

The nett result is therefore a version of the 8080 which spans a
wider range on the power spectrum. At the top end, its range of
application has been increased significantly. Since high volume
production is the secret of success in semiconductor manufacture,
the 8085 with its wider cover of the applications spectrum must bring
definite advantages to Intel. Whether or not the user will benefit
is yet to be seen.

The 8085 will, however, undoubtedly be used because it is so similar
to the 8080 that users are having no difficulty in changing over and
will want to do so, if only because of the single power supply voltage.
Bearing in mind the existence of the new Intel 8048 and 8748 at the
lower end of the spectrum and the fact that the 8085 does not incorporate the significant improvements which were included in the original
target specification, it is difficult to see why the 8085 was issued
in its present form.

It does not represent the sort of breakthrough which industry usually expects from Intel. Could it be that it is designed to act as a stop-gap until Intel finalises its 16 bit machine?

4.2.5   Intel 8048 and 8748

The 8048 is a single chip 8 bit microcomputer containing 1K bytes of ROM and 64 bytes of RAM. It is intended for the lower end of the application spectrum and in fact is remarkable in many ways. Although it is intended mainly for the single chip microcomputer area, it can be used with external memory. This represents a definite advantage over other single chip microcomputers since it would other- wise be very difficult to debug the system. The facility to use external memory (both ROM and RAM) is also useful in the case where a product grows with time and reaches the point when the application program no longer fits in internal memory.

The 8748 is perhaps even more remarkable since it contains an ultraviolet light erasable programmable ROM instead of mask programmed ROM. This makes it viable for small quantity production and enables field trials to be carried out before masks are made for the 8048 version. The most common criticism is that it is not software compatible with the 8080. Whether such compatibility is desirable can be debated; certainly the 8048/8748 contains several instructions, particularly in the bit handling area which are not available on the 8080. There are several variations on the 8048/8748, notably the 8035 which is an 8048 less internal ROM and the 8041 and 8741 which have minor changes to the bus structure so that they can act as intelligent peripherals to an 8080 or 8085 system.

4.2.6   Motorola 6800

The Motorola 6800 is in many ways very similar to the Intel 8080. It belongs to the single chip general purpose microprocessor class and is almost as much an industry standard as the 8080. There has been much debate as to which of the two is the better, but in fact there is probably very little to choose between them. The 6800 scores well in several areas: single power supply, more structured instruction set, more addressing modes, easier interfacing.

The 8080 on the other hand has more registers, better double precision arithmetic instructions and a more comprehensive interfacing structure. In general, if one has had experience of one, there is little point in changing to the other.

The 6800 was brought out later than the 8080 and was clearly designed to compete with it. Since it did not have to be compatible with an earlier microprocessor as did the 8080, Motorola was able to arrange the architecture so that a more orderly instruction set was possible.

For this reason, the 6800 is more readily understandable which accounts for its popularity amongst newcomers to the field. The interfacing is also easier to understand, since the signals available at the pins are conceptually simpler. The "valid-memory-address" (VMA) signal for example tells the outside world when the address lines contain a genuine address. Thus there is no need for status latches as are required on an 8080 system.

However, this simplified approach also has disadvantages. The reduced number of control lines makes it more difficult to do certain functions. There is for example no "wait-ready" handshake system to allow the use of slow memory. It is still possible to use slow memory, but to do so, the clock must be slowed down or temporarily switched off, which in turn brings other problems. Motorola publishes a very comprehensive application manual containing many circuit suggestions for carrying out such functions. The 6800 is backed by a wide range of support chips which make system design straightforward. Like the 8080, the whole family is compatible with TTL which means that there should be no difficulty in interfacing other logic to the family.

4.2.7 Motorola 6802

The 6802 is a new version of the 6800 which contains an internal clock generator and 128 bytes of RAM. In all other respects it is compatible with the 6800. The 6802 is designed to be compatible with the complete range of 6800 support chips, but is intended to be mainly used with the new 6486 to implement a two chip microcomputer.

The 6846 contains 2K bytes of ROM, an 8 bit bidirectional input-output port with two control lines and a 16 bit timer.

Such a two chip system is somewhat different to other competitive equivalents in that a standard easily expandable bus structure is used betwen the two chips. This obviously has definite attractions since it allows not only other 6800 family parts to be used, but also user designed specials.

The disadvantage of this is the heavy demand made on the pins needed for communication between the two chips. As a result there are only sufficient pins for a single byte of input-output as opposed to maybe three or four bytes on other two chip systems. Nevertheless the associated generality is very welcome, and it permits easy system expansion through the use of other family parts such as the 6820 peripheral interface adaptor.

4.2.8 Zilog Z80

The Z80 was designed by the same team that designed the 8080 and is based on the 8080. The instruction set contains all those of the 8080 and some additional ones which make it more powerful. 8080 programs will therefore run on the Z80 without modification, the only exception to this being that some of the flag operations will, in certain circumstances, cause an 8080 program to act slightly differently; the half carry and parity flags are those effected. Should such a problem occur though, it is usually easily solved with minor program modifications. The Z80 also contains additional registers and a somewhat simplified interfacing structure, which make it easier to use. Unfortunately, many of the instructions which were lacking on the 8080, and which 8080 programmers would like to have seen, are still lacking on the Z80. In fact the Z80 seems to have been extended in a rather arbitrary fashion. Some of the instructions are very advanced for microprocessors (eg. block instructions), others appear to be somewhat missing the point. There are for example 240 variations on the bit setting, clearing and testing instructions, but there is still no instruction to load the contents of the H and L registers from an address pointed to by H and L, as is often required in 8080 programming.

One fundamental omission also is the ability to read the interrupt
mode (which can be set by software). This means that in a highly
structured modular set of programs, one module cannot change the
interrupt mode and reinstate it later. (As is necessary in operating
systems, utilities and debugging routines.)

Nevertheless, the Z80 is more powerful than the 8080 and does incorporate some nice features. The main criticism is perhaps the same
as the one frequently levelled at the 8080; namely that it was
constrained to be compatible with an earlier processor. The Zilog
team have obviously done well in extending the 8080, but had they
started from scratch with a more orderly approach, one feels that
the end result would have been far superior to any other 8 bit
microprocessor available even today.

4.2.9 Fairchild F8

The F8 was originally introduced as a two chip microcomputer, with the
partitioning onto the two chips such that the ROM (designation 3851)
was basically on one chip and everything else on the other (designation
3850). In order to achieve this, and still leave enough pins for
other functions, two registers, the program counter and the memory
address register, were also placed on the ROM chip as were two
input-output ports and a timer. This meant that although the device
could not use standard ROM's a two chip configuration was possible,
which at the time of its introduction was very advanced. It was
intended for high volume applications and has been thus used on
several occasions. It owes its success to its very low price and to
the fact that not much else is needed in the way of additional hardware to make a working system. The instruction set is somewhat
primitive compared with the standard eight bit microprocessors, but
bearing in mind its price, and the fact that it offers a complete
microcomputer on two chips, it is quite acceptable. It would not be
suitable for low quantity production volumes in which the extra development cost involved in using the primitive instruction set is not offset by its low price. It is also available as a single chip microcomputer (3860) which makes it even more attractive in large volume
applications.

One point to watch is that Mostek's version, the 3870, uses a slightly different pin out, although it is software compatible.

4.2.10 National Semiconductor SC/MP

The SC/MP is an 8 bit single chip microprocessor. It contains a single accumulator in which all operations are performed and an extension register which is used as a temporary holding register. There are four 16 bit pointer registers, one of which is the program counter.   Subroutines are called by swapping the contents of one of the pointer registers with the program counter. If nested sub-routines are required the return address storage must be handled by software. The instruction set is very well laid out and simple to understand.   The instructions themselves are very basic and are not very efficient in terms of execution time or memory requirement. Since the SC/MP is fabricated in P-channel MOS which is a slow technology, the overall throughput of the processor is very low. However, because of its compactness and simple easy to understand architecture, it is well suited to applications at the lower end of the spectrum, especially if the application is to be implemented by inexperienced programmers.

It is also possible to link several SC/MP's together to implement a multiprocessor system.   Although interesting it would probably be better in most cases to choose a more powerful processor if the application cannot be satisfied with a single SC/MP.

4.2.11 Other 8 bit microprocessors

There are several more 8 bit microprocessors on the market although none of them has really had much market penetration. The Signetics 2650 and the MOS Technology 6502 are perhaps worth mentioning. Had it not been for the existence of the two industry standards, Intel and Motorola, these might have become quite popular.

The 6502 is one of a series of similar processors, intended to be an improved 6800 (rather as the Z80 relates to the 8080), but although very strong in its addressing capabilities, it suffers as does the 2650 from a somewhat inadequate instruction repertoire.

4.2.12 Rockwell PPS4 series

The Rockwell PPS4 and its two chip and one chip microcomputer derivatives (PPS4/2 and PPS4/1) are 4 bit machines which, because of the wide range of support chips are used fairly extensively. The architecture is however, fairly old and the competition from more modern devices is likely to result in their gradual demise. The PPS4 series, like the F8 owes much of its popularity to its price and compactness. It is difficult to program and has a rather rudimentary instruction set. Although it is a 4 bit device its application areas correspond mainly with those of the F8.

4.2.13 Other 4 bit microprocessors

Of the other 4 bit microprocessors available, the Texas Instruments TMS1000 and its derivatives are the most important. However, the general trend away from 4 bits means that interest in this and other 4 bit devices is fading. The main advantage of the TMS1000 is its extremely low price which makes it attractive for high volume low complexity tasks.

4.2.14 Intersil IM6100

This 12 bit microprocessor is important for two reasons, firstly it is one of the few CMOS microprocessors available, which makes it interesting for low power applications, and secondly it is compatible with the well established PDP8 minicomputer. This has the advantage that there is a range of established software packages already available but brings with it two problems.

Firstly the subroutine return address system used on the PDP8 does not lend itself readily to use with programs in ROM. (The return addresses are stored at the beginning of subroutines rather than on a stack). This means that either the programs have to be extensively modified, which negates the advantages brought by the compatibility, or the IM6100 has to be used with RAM only. This is only practical in a limited number of applications. The second problem is that one of the more useful options for the PDP8, the extended arithmetic element, which enhances the power of the PDP8 considerably, is not implemented in the IM6100. This very much reduces the range of applicability of the IM6100.

4.2.15 RCA Cosmac

The RCA Cosmac is also a CMOS microprocessor. It is based on a
rather unusual architecture with a bank of 16 registers each of which
is 16 bits wide. These registers are accessed by pointers which
have to be preset in much the same way as is done in the Intel 4004
and Fairchild F8. The program counter is one of these registers
and therefore subroutine calls can be performed by altering the
pointer so that another register is designated the program counter.
Although such an architecture is interesting, it does not lend itself
to a structured approach to programming, using modules and nested
subroutines. For small applications where low power consumption is
important, the Cosmac is, however, probably a good choice.

4.2.16 Texas Instruments 9900 series

The TMS9900 is one of a series of microprocessors recently brought
out by Texas Instruments. It is based on a 16 bit architecture
which is somewhat different to other microprocessors. In order to
save area on the chip, the registers are implemented in the main
memory. This means that the microprocessor can boast 16 registers
and although they are 16 bits wide, still have enough room on the
chip to implement an advanced instruction set. Had the registers been
on the chip, Texas Instruments would no doubt have had to economise
on either the instruction repertoire, or on the speed of the processor.

The architecture is somewhat unusual in that the 9900 has an on chip
pointer to the register bank in memory and a system whereby this pointer
can be saved in the register bank when a subroutine is called. The
only other registers on the chip are the program counter and the
status register. Both of these are also saved in the register bank
during a subroutine call. Thus 13 of the 16 registers are normally
available as general purpose registers. Another way of looking at
this is to regard the system as having a stack, of which the top 16
words are the general registers. When a subroutine is called another
16 words are added to the stack and the program counter etc. saved
in the normal manner. Since the position of these register banks can
be anywhere in memory, the stack should be considered as being scattered
throughout memory, rather than in contiguous locations.

The instruction set is powerful but contains the usual quirks. There are for example autoincrement indirect addressing instructions but no autodecrement ones. Hardware multiply and divide are included in the instruction set and it is refreshing to see these done correctly for a change, namely based on unsigned integers. Hardware multiply and divide is often arranged to work with signed numbers which makes it virtually useless for multiple precision arithmetic. It is, on the other hand, relatively easy to convert unsigned arithmetic to signed arithmetic with software.

The 990 is a TTL version of the 9900 which takes the form of a mini-computer. Its instruction set is compatible with the 9900 except in some minor areas which give it greater power. Although the 9900 is powerful as a microprocessor, one would normally expect a somewhat more elegant instruction set from a good minicomputer.

Texas Instruments are also extending the series in the other direc-tion towards the single chip microcomputer with several variations (c.f. Intel 8048). The main step in this direction is via the 9940, a single chip mask programmed device with good compatibility to the 9900. Since this has not yet actually been made available, it is still subject to change and therefore there is little point in describing it in detail. Suffice it to say that if Texas Instruments manage to make it on a commercially viable basis, and without too many specification reductions, then the other single chip manufac-turers will have a hard time ahead of them. Other variations planned for the near future include an ultra violet light erasable PROM version (c.f. Intel 8748).

4.2.17 Ferranti FlOOL

The FlOOL owes its fame to two assets. The first is that it is fabricated in a bipolar technology which immediately makes it interest-ing for military applications. The second, which may not be regarded as an asset outside the U.K., is that it is British. This has obvious political implications in the nationalised industries and in the defence area.

The fact that Ferranti have managed to implement a 16 bit single chip microprocessor in a bipolar technology is itself remarkable, since bipolar technologies are not normally considered suitable for high density chips (except I^2L). The choice of bipolar approach has however brought with it certain penalties.

In order to implement the processor in a bipolar technology, serial techniques have been used to keep the chip size reasonable. This has meant that the extra speed inherent in bipolar designs has been lost. The result is a chip with instruction speeds roughly comparable to MOS devices.

The architecture supports a single accumulator or general purpose register, and the instructions are fairly simple. This means that it does not have as high a performance as other 16 bit machines. It is however, of considerable interest for British and possibly Common Market military products.

One area where it scores well is in the associated interface chips. These are unique in concept to the FIOOL and do not have any parallel in the other 16 bit microprocessors. A typical FIOOL system is likely to use several of these which at first appear to greatly increase the total chip count. They do however, remove or at least greatly reduce the necessity for large quantities of standard SSI and MSI support chips for address decoding, etc. and they greatly simplify the hardware design. The resultant bus structure is somewhat different to the standard separate control, data and address bus idea, but it fits in with a 16 bit architecture which would otherwise require an excessive number of bus lines. However, it departs quite clearly from the minimum chip concept which seems to be the guiding rule of many of the other microprocessor manufacturers.

4.2.18 General Instruments CP1600

The CP1600 was one of the first 16 bit microprocessors to arrive on the market. It was modelled on the PDP11, although it departs quite a bit from the PDP11 architecture. In order to be able to implement the processor several compromises were made, in particular the generality associated with the choice of registers and addressing

modes which makes the PDP11 so attractive was forsaken. Although
the data handled is 16 bits wide, the instructions are only 10 bits
wide. This obviously leads to certain inefficiencies and inelegant
compromises.

4.2.19   National Semiconductor PACE

PACE is a 16 bit microprocessor which was derived from the IMP 16
series. Unfortunately, it has several basic limitations such as a
small stack which limits the amount of subroutine nesting possible,
and relatively low operation speed due to its P-channel MOS implementation. In terms of throughput and generality, it does not
compete with more modern 16 bit microprocessors.

The instruction set does however, contain several rather unusual and
interesting concepts, in particular in the various skip instructions.
These concepts are only directly applicable in processors like the
PACE in which all instructions are of a fixed number of bits (16 in
the case of PACE).

4.2.20   Digital Equipment Corporation LSI 11

The LSI 11 is a single board computer with an instruction set
compatible with the PDP 11. This means that it is very powerful,
particularly in view of the fact that an optional chip can be plugged
in to provide floating and fixed point arithmetic instructions.
Although the LSI 11 is somewhat more expensive than other similar
single board computers, it is ideally suited to low volume applications because the range of support available for the PDP 11 series
can be used on the LSI 11. The architecture, on which several other
computers have been modelled, includes eight general purpose 16 bit
registers, one of which is the program counter and one of which is
the stack pointer. All the registers can be used in a variety of
ways with a range of very powerful addressing modes. The LSI 11 card
itself includes 4K words of RAM and a debugging routine implemented
in microcode (a variation of DEC's ODT program). The implementation
of the LSI 11 is based on the use of a microprogrammable microprocessor developed as a custom circuit for DEC by Western Digital,
who originally intended to make it available with other microprograms
to emulate other computers. The recent financial involvement of DEC
in Western Digital could result in this development not proceeding.

4.2.21 Akers MIPROC

The Akers MIPROC, probably better known through its second source Plessey, is a very fast 16 bit single board computer. It is included here because of its high throughput as an indication of the sort of performance that can be achieved. MIPROC uses separate data and program memories for speed. Although the instruction set is not particularly sophisticated, the fact that it executes most of its instruction set in 350 us means that its throughput is about 10 times that of the 8080. Hardware multiply and divide are included in the basic instruction set. The instruction set can be extended be an option which provides a much improved addressing capability through the use of an index register.

MIPROC is implemented in Schottky TTL which makes it suitable for military applications, as well as giving it high speed.

4.2.22 Microprogrammable multi-chip microprocessors (bit slice)

There is a range of microprogrammable multi-chip microprocessors on the market known as "bit slice", the most commonly used ones being the Intel 3000 series and the AMD 2900 series. They all differ from the microprocessors described so far in that before they can be used, the basic architecture and instruction set of the processor have to be designed. In other words they are building blocks from which microprocessors can be made. They are usually controlled by a micro-program which determines the characteristics of the final machine an as such are not intended for first time users of microprocessors. The characteristics of any microprocessor based on them will depend on the way in which they are used. Their main application area is in implementing fast controllers or very flexible computers in special-ised areas.

4.2.23 The Intel 8086

There are three main contenders in the 16 bit market. The Intel 8086 16 bit microprocessor which will execute 8080 and 8085 software if it is put through a translator program at source level. It has an advanced instruction set with many facilities not seen previously on microprocessors such as dynamic relocation and segmentation of pro-grams, ASCII BCD and binary arithmetic and a large number of registers.

It is available ex-stock and is clearly designed to compete with large minicomputers on their own ground.

It uses HMOS process technology and is contained in a 40 pin package. Intel claim that it will execute programs between seven and twelve times faster than the 8080, and that programs will be up to 25% shorter in length. The device is supported by the Intellec Series II development system.

4.2.24 The Motorola 68000 (MACS) and 6909

Preliminary information has been received on MACS, the Motorola Advanced Computer System, which is alternatively known as the 68000. This device is likely to be contained in a 64 pin package direct memory addressing for 64M bytes using a 24 bit address bus; it has been indicated that there will be approximately 60 instruction types with a wide range of addressing modes. It is understood that modules are under development in order that the EXORcisor system can be used to support the device.

Motorola's 6809 device, which is presently available, can be said to bridge the gap between 8 bit and truly 16 bit devices. It uses a 16 bit internal operation but an 8 bit bus structure. It is probably best classified as a really good 8 bit processor with many 16 bit operations. It out-classes all other 8 bit devices, but does not compete with modern 16 bit processors.

4.2.25 The Zilog Z8000

Zilog's 16 bit device has been named the Z8000. It is software compatible with the Z80 and the company claims that its design has been influenced by the better facilities of the IBM 370 and DEC PDP-11 computer systems. Its instruction set includes 110 instruction types. Direct addressing up to 8M bytes will be facilitated using an external memory management chip. Two versions will in fact be available; the 8M bytes version will be contained in a 48 pin package, and a 40 pin package will provide direct addressing to 64K bytes. Zilog have indicated that a new development system is being designed. Like the Intel 8086, it contains many advanced features and is very similar in concept but very different in detail.

An agreement has been made between Zilog and AMD under which AMD
will second source the Z8000 and the two companies will jointly
develop and cross license the peripheral and support chips.

4.2.26 Comments on the New Microprocessors

Industry has been awaiting the arrival of the latest generation of
16 bit microprocessors for some time mow, and the recent arrival of
the Intel 8086 is regarded by many as a great step forward. There
have of course been 16 bit devices on the market for some time, but
these have not offered the same performance, ease of programming,
suitability for high level languages or ease of use as the Intel 8086.

Of the previous generation, the only 16 bit processor of any real
significance was the Texas Instruments 9900. Texas Instruments
managed, through the rather neat approach of putting the registers in
main memory, to implement a 16 bit device and get it on the market
two years ahead of the latest devices. As commented earlier though
the 9900 suffers from a rather unusual architecture (liked by some)
and it will probably lose a large proportion of its market to the
new 16 bit devices which are more conventional and better in most
respects.

Hot on the tail of the Intel 8086 is the Zilog Z8000. This device
is very similar to the 8086 as far as the general architecture and
types of instruction are concerned. On comparing the two, one gets
the impression that Zilog's marketing department had a greater
involvement in the design of the Z8000 than the Intel's marketing
department had in the 8086, since the Z8000 contains a larger number
of features likely to impress the semi-expert. These include such
things as an 8M byte rather than a 1M byte address space and
32 x 32 bit instead of 16 x 16 bit multiplications. Intel on the
other hand, have concentrated on other less eye catching but equally
important aspects of the design. Zilog's product is still subject to
alteration and so may still end up the better product, but Intel have
the advantage of being first on the market.

Overall it is difficult to say at the moment, without the experience of anything but small programming exercises, which of the two is the best choice; something which will depend to a large extent on the support offered.

Motorola has traditionally lagged behind Intel and Zilog as far as getting to the market first is concerned. They have a habit though, of getting the product right, so that when it eventually arrives, it takes its proper share of the market. The Motorola 6809, though talked about as a 16 bit processor is better classed as a much improved 6800. When viewed in this light, the 6809 must be regarded as a significant step forward in the 8 bit arena. It contains excellent addressing facilities, as did MOS-Technology's earlier attempted improvement of the 6800, namely the 6502, as well as more registers, and an improved instruction set. There had not been significant announcement in the 8 bit area since the Z80 was announced many years ago. The 6809 is a very welcome development in the 8 bit market. It enhances the 6800 range much more than the 8080 range has been enhanced by the 8085.

4.3   Microprocessor suppliers

Some general background information on device suppliers is important to users, particularly with respect to their size and market share, since this is indicative of the extent of on-going product development and support; one of the most important factors in choosing a micro-processor.

4.3.1 The development of the market

When the first commercial microprocessors were introduced in 1972 many organisations were reluctant to use them. The difficulties in manufacturing LSI components were much talked of, and many would-be users hesitated to invest substantial amounts of design effort or to base their products on this key component. There was clearly a possibility that Intel would not be able to reliably produce sufficient production quantities and that there would be no alternative source. As a result, a year elapsed before designers began to commit themselves and another year passed before designs incorporating microprocessors began to emerge into production.

However, far from there being the difficulties in purchasing microprocessors which many anticipated, the period 1973-1975 saw a rapid proliferation of devices, a rapid growth in formal and informal second sources, and a large number of companies competing to obtain a firm foothold in the market place. Since then there has been a rationalisation in the industry, only a few companies have achieved significant market shares and a small number now dominate the market place. As a result while there are approximately 150 devices available from about 40 suppliers, in fact the number of commercially significant devices is very much less.

The supply situation is of course dominated by U.S. companies. Largely, by being first, but also by pursuing a very effective product development and marketing programme, Intel has emerged as the leader. Motorola on the other hand has invested a very substantial amount in a massive marketing and promotional campaign which has enabled it to substantially catch up with Intel. As a result these two companies now have about 70% of the market in terms of users (see Figure 4.3-1). The remaining 30% market share is shared by approximately 40 suppliers.

In fact, Motorola presently appears to be slackening the pressure in its push to achieve parity with Intel. Although, with Intel's 8080, the 6800 is clearly an industry standard, there have been few announcements since late 1976 of new products from Motorola.

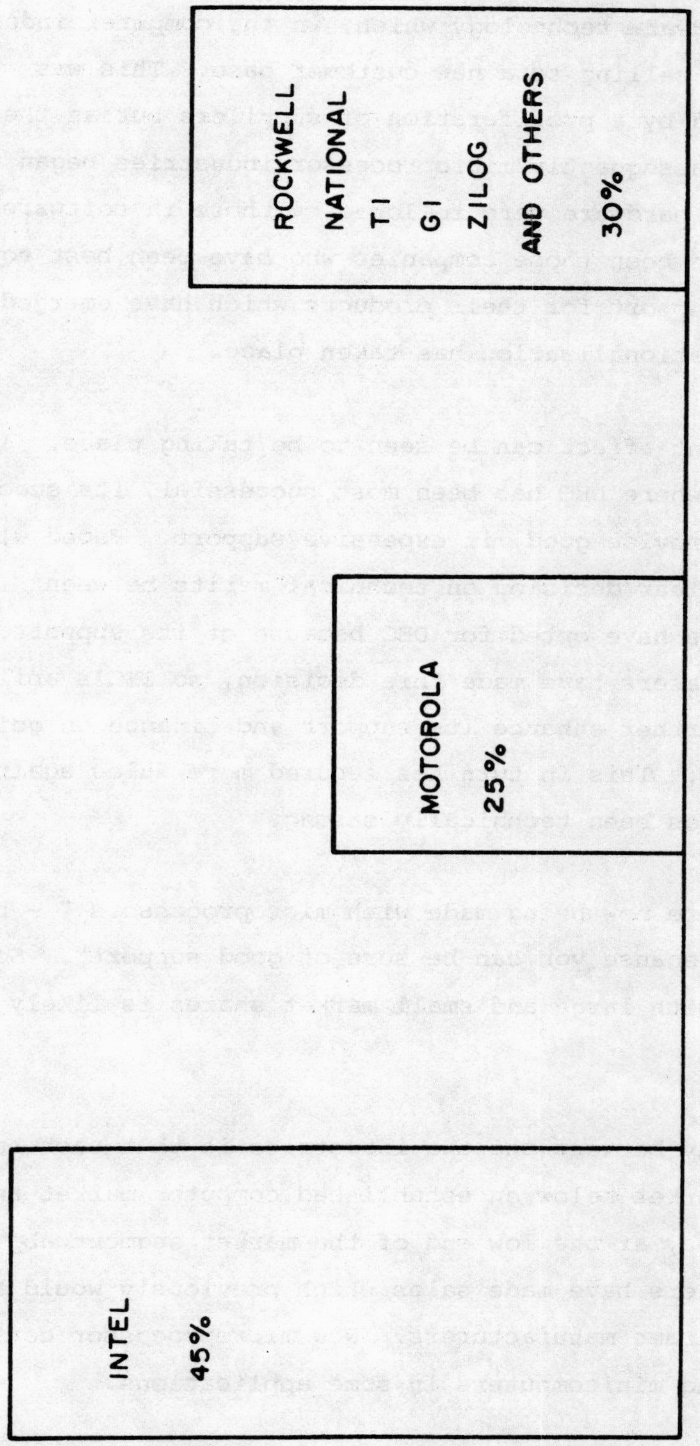

INTEL
45%

MOTOROLA
25%

ROCKWELL
NATIONAL
TI
GI
ZILOG
AND OTHERS

30%

FIG. 4.3-1 THE USER MARKET IN TERMS OF THE NUMBER OF COMMITTED FOLLOWERS.

4.3.2 Comparison with the minicomputer market

The microprocessor industry can be said to have followed a similar growth pattern to that for minicomputers. Initially there was a breakthrough in hardware technology which, in the computer industry, found new suppliers selling to a new customer base. This was immediately followed by a proliferation of suppliers but as the minicomputer and subsequently microprocessor industries began to mature, advances in hardware were followed by those in software and support. And it has been those companies who have been best equipped to establish full support for their products which have emerged when the shake-out and rationalisation has taken place.

Now another important effect can be seen to be taking place. In the minicomputer field, where DEC has been most successful, its success has enabled it to provide good, if expensive support. Faced with perhaps a not too clear decision on technical merits between computers, customers have opted for DEC because of its support. As more and more purchasers have made this decision, so DEC's ability has increased to further enhance its support and finance on going product development. This in turn has secured more sales against competition which has been technically strong.

Similar decisions are now being made with microprocessors " - buy Intel or Motorola because you can be sure of good support". So the gap between those with large and small market shares is likely to get even wider.

One other similarity between the two industries is that each has introduced a new market below an established computer market and then proceeded to eat away at the low end of the market segment above it. Minicomputer suppliers have made sales which previously would have gone to small mainframe manufacturers. Now microprocessor centred equipment is ousting minicomputers in some applications.

4.3.3 Market leaders

Whilst we can say in broad terms who the market leaders are, it is very difficult to rank suppliers and quantify their market shares. One reason is that the market is so new that the generation of related statistics is difficult, requiring a significant investment of effort, so that this form of information is not generally available. Another important reason is that to identify market shares one should perhaps define the market area and this is not so clear cut as one might imagine. For example, an organisation could determine its market share in terms of the total number of parts sold or the value of parts sold, or the total number of committed end users. An organisation could consider itself a leading supplier of 8-bit single chip devices; another may be significant in the group selling 16-bit microprocessors. One can also compare the relative significance of the companies supplying devices which are software compatible with microcomputers. A commonly adopted measurement relates to the number of committed followers to each supplier. As we have said, Intel and Motorola have 70% of the market in these terms. Rockwell, National, Texas Instruments, General Instruments and Zilog are significant among the remainder of suppliers.

4.3.4 Entry of Japanese suppliers

Although American companies have so far dominated the industry, one can perhaps anticipate that in the future leading suppliers could come from Japan. In 1976 a consortium was formed between leading manufacturers including NEC, Hitachi, Fujitsu, Toshiba, Mitsubishi and government laboratories to form the base for a concerted attack on the semiconductor industry by the early 1980's. In addition to numerous second sourcing agreements with U.S. companies, Japanese industry produces 4, 8, 12 and 16-bit devices for its home market. But its targetted developments in microprocessor and memory technology are set to achieve parity or even overtake the U.S. competition.

4.4 The basis for choosing a microprocessor

The preceding comments have covered a range of topics designed to bring out those factors which need to be considered in the final choice. This choice involves the establishment of priorities or weightings for these factors and a trade off of the characteristics of a microprocessor against them, since there is no one microprocessor which suits all applications or situations. Applications of course differ greatly in the requirements that they place on the micro-processor, and so before a microprocessor is chosen it is worth considering what characteristics are likely to be of greatest importance in the particular application.

In most applications the following will need to be considered:

- cost (of the microcomputer)
- performance (processing power)
- flexibility
- ease of use
- manufacturer's support
- reliability
- existence of second source suppliers
- power consumption
- range of complementary hardware
- special environmental constraints

4.4.1 Cost

The cost of the microprocessor itself is only important in very small systems, particularly single chip microcomputer systems. For very simple chips, such as the Texas Instruments TMS 1000, prices can be as low as £1 or £2 for very large quantities.

By contrast, the well established single chip microprocessors, such as the Intel 8080, cost about £20 in small quantities, falling to perhaps half that figure for 1000 up quantities. A typical system will however require many additional chips, including say 2 k bytes of RAM, i.e. 16 chips at about £2 each, and 2 k bytes of ROM at about £15. Thus, the memory alone is likely to cost two to three times as much as the microprocessor chip. Add to this the cost of the clock generator, input-output chips, power supply, printed circuit boards, etc. and the result is that the microprocessor accounts for only about 10% of the total component costs. When the assembly costs and a proportion of the design costs are included, the cost of the microprocessor itself becomes insignificant.

For this reason, with this middle microprocessor class it is usually better to base the design on an overpowerful microprocessor. The extra power will often result in reduced development costs and lower memory requirements.

This contrasts with the single chip microcomputer class where production volumes are traditionally high, development costs unimportant and the cost of the microcomputer significant. Here the cheapest microcomputer may well be preferable, despite the inconvenience and cost of the additional programming effort required.

At the top end of the spectrum, things are not quite so clear. The cost of the microprocessor is likely to be very much higher and the component cost for a bipolar microprogrammable chip set, including the microcode ROM, may well be about £200. However, performance rather than cost is usually the most important characteristic of such systems. Whether the £200 component cost is significant will depend on the cost of the other parts of the system. These by implication are also likely to be expensive, if the total system is proportioned correctly so as to make use of the high throughput of a bipolar microprogrammable chip set. One point to bear in mind is that such systems are difficult to design, so that unless production volumes are high, development costs are likely to be significant. The most economical course is then to choose the best chip set and keep the development costs proportionately low, as in the case of the single chip microprocessor.

4.4.2 Performance

The performance, processing power or throughput capability of a microprocessor is very difficult to define rigorously but is usually taken to mean the speed at which a task can be completed. Factors which influence throughput include the clock rate, the bit length, the number of registers and the instruction variety and elegance. When the microprocessor is built into a microcomputer, additional factors can influence the system throughput. These include the memory speed, the programming language used and the availability of suitable peripherals.

The throughput of two or more processors is usually compared using benchmark tests in which test programs are written for each and used to estimate the relative speeds of execution. Since execution speeds are application dependent, such benchmarks are only an approximate indication of the throughput capability.

In most applications the throughput capability should be far higher
than is really necessary. This leaves room for expansion, allows
modifications to be made, and most important of all, allows greater
use of sophisticated programming techniques, (high level languages,
macros, structured programming, decision tables, etc.) which in turn
bring higher reliability, easier programming and increased flexibility.
As the throughput required approaches the capability of the microcomputer, programming becomes increasingly difficult, which in turn
results in higher development costs. As a general guideline, the
throughput required should not exceed 50% of that which the microcomputer can handle, the exception being in cost reduced (single chip)
high volume applications.

4.4.3 Flexibility

If the systems flexibility is important then a high level language
should be used, or at least a well structured, modularised assembler
program. Generally speaking, single chip microcomputers are not very
flexible in use compared with single chip microprocessors. The
latter, if based on a standardised bus, can be reconfigured by
swapping peripherals and altering input-output routines. The ultimate
in flexibility is probably achieved through the use of a minicomputer
but of course this is an extreme solution and not within the scope of
this section.

4.4.4 Ease of use

An experienced programmer can learn how to program a different microprocessor effectively in a week or two. It can however take
considerably longer to learn how to use the various support programs
and associated equipment and to learn the conventions used by a
different manufacturer. A change between microprocessors of the same
manufacturer is therefore easier than a change between different
manufacturers.

The medium complexity microprocessors, such as the single chip microprocessors, tend to be easiest to program. The simpler single chip
microcomputers however usually have inelegant instruction sets which
make them awkward to use. For this reason they should not be used
for very low volume applications. Microprogrammable bit slice

microprocessors are difficult to use unless the microprogram which
defines the instruction set has already been written. In this case
they can be as easy to use as a minicomputer. Obviously the ease
with which a given microprocessor can be programmed depends very
much on the support available with it. This is usually a more
decisive factor than the characteristics of the microprocessor itself.
The implication of this is that one should choose a microprocessor
from an established supplier with a proven level of support.

4.4.5 Manufacturer's support

Manufacturer's support covers the provision of a range of services
from the development system and its associated software through to
documentation, maintenance of the development system and providing
answers to technical queries. Many manufacturers operate through
distributors in the U.K. so that the support they offer is probably
as important as that of the manufacturers. The importance of good
support has already been stressed.

4.4.6 Reliability

There is very little data available yet about the reliability of
microprocessors and associated components, and that which is available
has not shown any great differences between such devices and other
integrated circuits of comparable technologies and complexities, with
the possible exception of pattern sensitivity. This can occur in
memories, where repeated writing into one cell influences data in
neighbouring cells and in microprocessors themselves, where certain
sequences of instructions interact in an unwanted manner. Whether
such instruction sensitivity occurs, is the subject of much discussion
but instances have been observed in prototype microprocessors and it
is reasonable to assume that it is not impossible in production
versions of such chips. Unfortunately, it is impractical to test all
combinations of all instructions in order to test against such
instruction sensitivity. Pattern sensitivity in memories is more
common and exhaustive testing, although slow and expensive, is sometimes done. It was prevalent in early 4 k dynamic RAM's, but later
designs seem to have improved in this respect.

In practice, failures are most likely to occur in the soldered joints and interconnections between chips, so that the reduced number of chips usually obtained by basing a design on microprocessors rather than on other implementation methods leads to a comparatively high reliability. This is of course especially true at the lower end of the spectrum where only one or two chips are required.

4.4.7 Second source suppliers

Most of the major microprocessors are now made by more than one manufacturer. Some of these second source devices are the result of mask exchange agreements between suppliers, others are unofficial "Chinese copies". Although complete compatibility is only obtainable with true mask exchange second sources, the unofficial copies are more independent and therefore less likely to be influenced by the marketing policies of the original firm.

Unfortunately, with one or two notable exceptions, many of the microprocessor suppliers are based on the St. Andreas fault line, so a major earthquake which is a distinct possibility in the next few years, could wipe out all the sources of several of the main microprocessors! A change in American export legislation, although unlikely, could also restrict supplies so that many users may conclude that the best type of second source is one based in a different country and run by a different manufacturer.

4.4.8 Power consumption

The power consumption of most commonly available single chip microprocessors and microcomputers usually lies between 0.5 and 1 W. Other system components must of course be considered when calculating the total power consumption, in particular memory chips and clock generator chips. If low power consumption is necessary I^2L or CMOS parts should be used. The advantage in using them however is lost if they are operated at full speed. Power can also be conserved by switching sections of the microcomputer off (under computer control) when not in use, or by using the standby feature available on some memories and microprocessors, when data must be conserved.

4.4.9 Range of complementary hardware

For some applications the existence of a good range of compatible chips to support the microprocessor may be important. Comments on this aspect have been made earlier in 4.2.

4.4.10 Special environmental constraints

The existence of special requirements, such as military specifications or minimum physical size and weight, may well be overriding factors for certain tasks. In this case the decision is often an easy one and may be Hobson's choice.

4.4.11 Conclusions

Fortunately for most users the choice of a particular supplier or processor is not in fact as difficult as it may appear. For example, in a navigational system for a civil aircraft, processing power, reliability and physical size and weight might be considered as most important. The choice might in this case be a tailor-made micro-programmed system which would be expensive and difficult to program. In a domestic environment, ease of programming might be the most important characteristic.

It is usually possible to look at a potential application and decide what type it is in general terms, for example, a low speed, high reliability military application involving mainly logical operations, or a medium speed industrial application in an area of high competition and medium production volumes. Based on such a description one can usually make a fairly good choice of processor type. The two hypothetical examples quoted above would probably be best satisfied with a short bit length, bipolar microprogrammed chip set (possibly in I^2L technology) and a single chip microprocessor respectively. Having narrowed the choice of microprocessor down this much, the final choice is usually a matter of personal preference, or at least can be made on secondary considerations.

SECTION 5

THE DEVELOPMENT PROCESS

5.0   <u>THE DEVELOPMENT PROCESS</u>

This section describes the various stages in the development of a microprocessor based product, although the discussion is confined to those
aspects which differ significantly from conventional product development.
The main differences are due to the intrusion of software development
into the project. Software brings with it a tremendous increase in
flexibility which, however, makes it difficult to specify the system
requirements; it also brings problems in acquiring suitably experienced
personnel to implement the design and to manage the project. Management
of the project is made difficult by the fact that software is somewhat
illusory and neither easy to estimate nor monitor. It is therefore
important that the project is carefully planned and that the plan incorporates milestones and regular progress reviews. Breaking the project
down into phases is very desirable since it assists in the monitoring of
progress. The most important phases are discussed in detail in the
following paragraphs.

Throughout this discussion it has been assumed that the project is fairly
small, since a typical microprocessor development project usually requires
between 2K and 4K bytes of memory. The newcomer to the field is not
advised to undertake projects much larger than this initially, since almost
all entrants to the field comment after their first project that they
would do a second one differently and be able to avoid the many traps
commonly encountered.

5.1   <u>System requirements specification</u>
One of the most difficult tasks facing the first time user of a microprocessor, or indeed someone subcontracting work to an outside organisation
or internal microprocessor system development department, is specifying
the requirements of the product to be designed. On the one side, there
are the broad objectives of the original concept and on the other, the
technically and economically feasible solutions.   The final implementation
is usually a compromise between that which is feasible and that which is
desirable. With conventional products, the marketing department or the
originator of the basic requirement have learnt to ask for products which
are likely to be both technically and economically feasible.

Microprocessors, however, have upset this pattern of development, since
they offer so many possibilities that most people do not know what to ask

for.   In contrast to conventional systems, extra processing facilities can often be built in without increasing the manufacturing costs, but on the other hand adding an extra input or output can sometimes increase the costs disproportionately.

A closer than normal cooperation is therefore required between the marketing department (the customer) and the microprocessor engineering department (the system supplier).   A formula which has been found to work well, at least with small systems, is for the 'customer' and 'supplier' to work out a formal target requirement specification jointly, based on a much less detailed list of objectives determined by the 'customer'.   The preliminary specification as supplied by the 'customer' should be divided into the essential required features and the desirable features.   A good engineering department will then be able to suggest enhancements to the product which the 'customer' had not dared ask for and can also question the necessity of features which cause problems when using microprocessors.

The target specification resulting from this discussion should include all the essential features and as many of the desirable features as are economically and technically feasible.   It is also likely to include a list of features which are desirable but need more detailed study before they are included.   The final requirements specification therefore usually emerges later in the project after the outline design phase (see 5.3).

As an example of this procedure, the 'customer' who requires a microprocessor based petrol pump controller might specify that he wants it to record and display the petrol dispensed, calculate and display the total price and, if possible, issue the correct number of trading stamps.   The engineering department might in time suggest that additional features such as the automatic calculation of discounts for cash payment, calculation of the change due etc., could be incorporated very cheaply and that, while the stamp dispenser is an expensive mechanical addition, it would be much cheaper to display the number of stamps due along with the total price. Other trade-offs might be made when the number of inputs and outputs required are examined.   In this way a good compromise can often be reached.

As in any other requirements specification, it is important to specify only what is to be done, and not how this is to be implemented.   The choice of microprocessor, the division between hardware and software etc., are best left out of the specification under normal circumstances.   When the design has progressed somewhat, these details may have to be altered.

It is also important to specify what should happen in abnormal circumstances. It is for example not sufficient to state that a printer should
print a certain character on receipt of a certain code. The action to
be taken when the paper has run out must also be defined. Particularly
relevant in this context are the actions to be taken in the event of
operator error. Pressing both start and stop buttons together for example
should not cause the device to do anything undesirable, or at least unpredictable.   The specification of the action to be taken under abnormal
conditions is often overlooked as is the implementation of the subsequent
safeguards. This is one of the major causes of dissatisfaction of users
of microprocessor based products.

An excellent example of this was found in a program which was accessed
via a teletype. The 'ALT-MODE' key was not used in this application, but
if it was inadvertently pressed, it caused the system to crash with total
loss of all the data!   No one can accuse the program of not meeting its
specification since the action to be taken when normally unused keys were
pressed was almost certainly not even considered, let alone specified.
Such specification errors are unfortunately very common in many areas of
the whole of the computer industry.

5.2 Feasibility study

In most cases a separate feasibility study will not be necessary since
the broad approach to be taken will be considered (but not formally specified) during the specification phase. This is often adequate to obtain a
sufficiently positive indication that the system can be made within the
design constraints imposed.   Sometimes, however, there are tight constraints
on such features as the program execution time, memory size or physical
dimensions.   While it is fairly easy to estimate the approximate execution
time of a system and its physical size and weight, it is very difficult to
estimate the program size.

In fact, it is not normally the execution time of the whole program which
is of importance, but rather the execution time of a small critical loop,
which typically accounts for less than 20% of the total program. A short
feasibility study will permit the designer to actually write the program
for this critical loop and thereby determine its execution time.   It is
sufficient to write an 'approximate' program which may contain small
errors, without affecting the validity of the result. Since execution

speed is presumably critical, such a loop will not contain many sub-routine calls and will therefore not be dependent on other parts of the program.

An 'approximate' hardware design will likewise enable the designer to estimate the number of components to within one or two chips, thereby permitting the physical size and weight as well as the power consumption to be estimated, except that the largest unknown is the program size which determines how many memory chips are needed.

There is unfortunately no simple and reliable way of estimating the approximate program size - other than by tripling the designer's guess! The best way to estimate the program size is probably to compare the application with other systems and to try and identify something of about the same complexity. It is sometimes fruitful to break the total problem down into very small parts and to estimate the sizes of the parts individually. The errors unfortunately tend to accumulate rather than cancel.

Another reason for having a feasibility study might be to gain confidence in microprocessors. Such so called feasibility studies are however really training exercises. They are only feasibility studies in the sense that the feasibility of carrying out microprocessor design work with the resources available is being examined.

If the project is a large one or if it depends on some rather tenuous concepts for its success, then of course a feasibility study is warranted. The feasibility study then takes the form of a complete prototype design, leading to a demonstration model. A separate design exercise leading to a preproduction prototype can then be undertaken in the normal manner.

It should be possible at the end of this phase to freeze the final detailed requirements specification and to estimate the technical and commercial viability of the whole project. However, it is often useful to delay the freezing of the final requirements specification until the outline design has been done. This avoids unnecessary last minute negotiations about specification changes and permits a better trade-off between technical, economic and market requirements.

5.3 Outline design

The object of the outline design phase is to decide upon the broad approach to be taken and to settle the major design choices. To a large extent, this phase would overlap with the feasibility study if there were one.

5.3.1 Class of microprocessor

The first question to be settled is the general class of microprocessor which will be used. The factors governing this are the intended production volume and the complexity of the problem. For high volume, low complexity applications (e.g., a washing machine controller), one of the single chip microcomputers would probably be the most suitable, whereas for low volume high complexity applications a much easier to use and more powerful and flexible microprocessor is required. (See Section 4.1 on classes of micro-processor and Section 4.4 on the selection process.) Although it is not necessary to choose the actual type of microprocessor to be used, it is necessary to decide on the general class early on so that other decisions can be made. In particular, the approximate division between hardware and software should be decided at about the same time as choosing the micro-processor class. A survey of the different manufacturers' support chips will then often reveal one or two actual microprocessor types which are supported by other chips, suitable for use in the project. Often such considerations will point strongly to one particular type of microprocessor.

5.3.2 Microprocessor occupancy

In positioning the boundary between the hardware and software, the loading on the microprocessor must be considered. It is sometimes necessary to ensure that the reaction time of the system is adequate to meet the real time environmental requirements. Certain operations are rather slow when performed with a microprocessor and if there are many such functions to be performed it is likely that some will have to be implemented in hardware. To estimate whether this is necessary, it is useful to consider the 'microprocessor occupancy'. This is the amount of time which is used by a program divided by the total time available.

If, for example, a program takes 30 ms to run and the required reaction time is 100 ms then the microprocessor occupancy of this program is 0.3 or 30%. In order to keep the design easy the average microprocessor occupancy, considering all the different programs which need to be run, should not be more than about 50% and peaks greater than 80% should be avoided if possible. If higher values seem likely then the design is somewhat critical and a more powerful microprocessor should be considered or the hardware-software boundary moved. If the microprocessor occupancy is very low, either a simpler microprocessor can be used or much more done in software. In such a case, for example, serial transmission to a

teletype could be done using software, thereby saving a special purpose
UART chip. To actually estimate the microprocessor occupancy, a fairly
detailed flow diagram is required with an actual coding of the more
frequently executed parts.   Unfortunately, flow diagrams are often
neglected in small projects and are often regarded as a diversion rather
than as a help.

5.3.3 Hardware and software structure

The aim therefore in this outline design phase is to identify the major
hardware and software blocks and to obtain some estimates as to the magnitude of the problem and the most promising solution. Potential problems
should come to light at this stage and these should be investigated in
detail and solutions sought.   Any uncertainty in the feasibility of the
project should be resolved by the end of this phase. The actual work
involved will of course depend on the application, but it may take up
to 30% of the total design effort. At the end of this phase the structure
of both the hardware and software should be known as should the operational
and functional characteristics. These should include a fairly detailed
breakdown of the input and output lines needed, the types of facilities
which the user will have, the approximate execution times in a real time
system, the accuracies to which calculations are to be performed and the
complete breakdown of the solution into its constituent parts or modules,
both for the hardware and software.

As a last step in this phase the outline functional specification can be
written and milestones identified for the completion of the various parts
of the solution.

5.3.4 Documentation

The documentation which should be generated during this phase should
provide management with the first real opportunity to ensure that the
project is likely to meet the technical and economic design objectives.
This documentation should include the finalised system requirements
specification, the contents of which must be agreed upon by all concerned
and then 'frozen' before proceeding and outline flow diagrams showing how
the system is conceived.

Other documents which should be generated by the end of this phase, or
if possible earlier, are:

- the Module Test Specifications which are the test specifications used in verifying each of the modules. They would normally be written by the programmer to test his own modules.

- the System Test Specification which is written by the test department on a large project, and is used to ensure that the program sections each perform according to the overall system plan.

- the Acceptance Test Specification which is a formal document designed to test all aspects of the product to verify that the requirements specification is met. It would normally be written by the 'customer' in conjunction with the test department and is important in that a decision on whether the 'supplier' has met his formal obligations or not will be decided by whether the program passes the tests defined.

Specification revisions can be instigated at any time during the project by either the 'customer' or 'supplier' but only become effective if agreed by both parties.

5.4 Detailed design

Before starting the detailed design of the system it is useful to identify the design options which are most important. (Some of the programming trade-offs are shown in Fig.5.4-1.) Is it, for example, important that the software be ready quickly or is the final production cost the most important parameter? Is a high execution speed more important than low memory size? Are flexibility and transferability also important? Unfortunately, many of these options are mutually exclusive and therefore the designer is faced with the necessity to compromise. This should, however, be done consciously with the knowledge and agreement of management rather than by default. The choice of programming language is a dominant factor which influences these options considerably. A high level language will generally lead to a good deal of flexibility and transferability and be quick to implement, but will incur penalties in the program execution speed and size which will lead to higher production costs.

5.4.1 Modularity of design

In most cases the design should be kept highly modular so that it is easy to understand and modify. This leads to a small increase in memory size

PROGRAMMING TRADE-OFFS

1. THE TIME TAKEN TO WRITE THE PROGRAM

2. THE PROPORTION OF HARDWARE AND SOFTWARE

3. THE MEMORY REQUIRED FOR PROGRAM AND DATA

4. THE SPEED OF SYSTEM OPERATION

5. THE PROCESSING POWER OF THE COMPUTER

6. THE PROGRAM FLEXIBILITY

7. THE PROGRAM UNDERSTANDABILITY

8. THE CONFIDENCE THAT THE RESULT IS ERROR FREE

9. THE ABILITY AND EXPERIENCE OF THE PROGRAMMER(S)

10. THE FACILITIES AVAILABLE TO THE PROGRAMMERS

11. THE PROGRAMMING LANGUAGE.

FIG. 5·4-1 SOME PROGRAMMING DESIGN TRADE-OFFS

required and a medium increase in execution speed. In most cases the
resultant clarity, ease of programming and flexibility more than offset
these disadvantages. Even in assembler it is possible to incorporate
most of the philosophy of structured programming though of course the
detailed implementation of these principles is very different. One
very simple procedure which leads to reliable modular software is to consider the total problem to be composed of small modules linked together
in a hierarchical fashion. Each module should have a function which is
somehow related to a physical, easily definable function such as working
out averages, controlling a loop or printing. Each module should be self-
sufficient, relying only on those modules which it directly commands. In
order to complete this concept it is necessary to determine the responsibilities of the various modules and make sure they fulfil these
responsibilities.

For example, a module to print results should not be responsible for
doing anything but actually printing and communicating with the physical
printer according to commands that it receives. It is not the job of the
printer to decide on what should be printed. One of the major sources of
lack of clarity and subsequent failure of the system is the blurring of
such responsibilities. It is harder than one might at first imagine to
allocate the responsibilities of the modules. Whose responsibility is it,
for example, to take action when the physical printer runs out of paper?
On the one hand the main program which utilises the printer module should
not have to concern itself with such detail, on the other hand the
printer routine does not and should not have the necessary background
knowledge to decide whether to bring the whole process to a stop, inform
the operator and wait for the paper to be changed or just to ignore
further commands to print. In this particular example the most likely
solution is that the printer routine should politely notify this error
condition to the module immediately above it in the hierarchy. It has
then fulfilled its duty. The module above can then either take action
itself or inform its boss in turn. It is certainly not the job of any
module other than the printer module to interfere by directly communicating with the physical printer.

Once such a hierarchy has been decided upon and the responsibilities of
the modules allocated, the interfaces for communicating between modules
should be defined. These should be kept as simple as possible even

though this might make the modules themselves more complicated. The reason for this is that it pushes the detail down the hierarchy. The designer, writing modules at a particular level, need only concern himself then with the minimum amount of detail. If, for example, he wishes to print a character, it should be sufficient to call the printer module and hand over the character to be printed. When the printer module returns, it should report either 'done' or 'run out of paper'. The division of responsibilities is clear and the communication simple. If the designer writing the higher module has to concern himself with the details of the actual physical printer being used, or if he has to set up a complicated dialogue with the printer routine, then he will be distracted from implementing the higher module properly.

5.4.2 Flow diagrams

In order to actually plan such a hierarchy, it is useful to draw a flow diagram of each module on a separate piece of paper. Modules such as the printer module are simply put into a box and left until later. Many first time programmers, (if they draw flow diagrams at all) draw one enormous diagram in full detail on a size A1 sheet of paper. This is almost as confusing and just as useless as a road map of England showing every street. What are required are maps with different levels of detail. If this hierarchical approach is adopted and the responsibilities and interfaces carefully defined, the actual programming will be straightforward. Such techniques are already used in hardware design. An overall block diagram is used to show the basic structure of the total system, and each of the blocks such as the memory, the disc controller etc. taken in turn and its major parts shown on separate pieces of paper. The interfacing between the various parts is usually also kept simple so that modules can be easily used and interchanged. Somehow, these principles are not always adopted in software writing.

In the testing phase each of the modules should be tested individually since in any practical system it is impossible to adequately test the whole system at once. There are bound to be conditions which are not tested if the modules are not separately tested. It is also worth remembering that testing can only prove the presence of errors, never their absence.

5.4.3 <u>Documentation</u>

Three basic forms of document should be generated in the detailed design
phase and depending on the size and complexity of the project, other forms
of documentation may be desirable.

As a minimum though, descriptions are required of how the system functions,
how well it performs and how to use it.   The three documents required are:

- The System Implementation Description which is written as
  implementation proceeds and should contain sufficient information to enable a competent person not directly concerned with
  the project to rapidly understand how the system was implemented.
  It should therefore contain a description of the underlying
  principles on which the implementation is based and both outline
  and detailed descriptions of the way in which the software works.

  The most usual way of doing this is with flow diagrams. These
  should be augmented with specifications of all the modules,
  blocks and subroutines used. Listings of the programs should be
  included and should themselves contain carefully thought out
  comments. Note that it is not a good idea to comment every
  statement with a description of what that statement does; this
  is obvious to anyone who is competent enough to make use of the
  listing anyway, and is counterproductive since the important
  comments are lost in the detail. It is better to define what
  happens at the beginning of a section of code and only comment
  the less obvious points in the main body of the code. This way
  they stand out better.

- The Performance Specification which is a description of what the
  system does. It differs from the requirements specification in
  that it contains a detailed description of exactly which inputs
  and outputs etc. are used for the required functions and describes how the system works.   For example, the requirements
  specification might say 'user errors should be indicated to the
  user' and the performance specification might say 'the lamp
  labelled 'Error' will light for 10 s if any of the following user
  errors are encountered .....'.   The performance specification
  should also give actual performance values where the requirements
  specification included an upper or lower bound. For example, if

the requirements specification states that the system must respond within 10 ms, the performance specification might say that the response time is 7.5 ms.

- User manuals which should be written for most systems and should consist of several parts, namely operator manuals which describe the operation of the system very concisely, course material to explain to new users of the system how to use the system and detailed technical descriptions of how the system works. The first and third of these can often be derived from the performance specification. It is important not to mix these together as is usually done (Ref. several leading microprocessor manufacturers' assembler manuals).

5.5 Project costing and management

Managing a microprocessor based project is, at least superficially, no different to managing any other type of development project. As such it involves the four basic management functions of planning, motivating, monitoring and controlling. It is the purpose of this section to describe the ways in which microprocessor based projects require different management techniques rather than to describe these basic functions.

The three main additional problems facing the microprocessor project manager are first obtaining and retaining suitably experienced staff, secondly, estimating the magnitude of the software problem and thirdly, monitoring the progress of the software.

5.5.1 Use of formal documentation

One step towards easing the effect of these problems is to enforce higher than normal standards of documentation. The effect of this is to discipline the team members to record their design ideas. This usually means that greater thought is given to the whole design approach, something which normally leads to better software; it certainly improves the chances of replacement staff carrying on the project in the event of original team members leaving. Good documentation of this design approach also assists in the estimation of the overall complexity and of course helps throughout the project since it provides the only means to monitor progress, the output from programmers being essentially invisible.

5.5.2 Estimating the costs and monitoring progress

Estimating the amount of hardware required and its subsequent cost is fairly straightforward. This has already been discussed in 5.2 under Feasibility Studies.

Estimating the costs of the engineering effort involved in developing the system is more difficult. It was noted, however, in the ERA User Survey, that the breakdown of effort into separate tasks was fairly consistent. It is, therefore, worth looking at these figures in detail. (See Figure 5.5-1). Analysis and planning accounted on average for about 14% of the total effort, hardware design for about 12% and about 23½% was spent generating the software. This amounts to almost 50% of the total effort. The rest, apart from a small allocation for documentation, is typically taken up by testing and evaluation. Testing is, of course, often a polite word for finding out why the system does not work and putting it right. As such it is a necessary if time consuming part of the project.

It is clear from the breakdown of effort that the projects included in this survey included a significant proportion of special hardware (hardware testing was 19.8% and greater than the software proportion). Making due allowance for this fact, the percentage breakdown forms a useful guide for an initial estimate or can provide a means of checking one's own first assessment.

Progress can to a certain extent be monitored against these typical breakdown figures. This must however be done with caution because it has been found in practice that to write the first 90% of a program takes 90% of the estimated time - and so does the remaining 10%!

5.5.3 Estimating software

An estimate for software is more difficult, but the user survey results already quoted above provide a means of assessment. This showed an average software production effort of 50.6 man weeks to which should be added half the effort dedicated to problem analysis and documentation giving a final total for software production of 61.5 man weeks. The average program size (ROM + PROM only) was 4.3k bytes which gives a typical production rate of 1.9 bytes/h. However, when estimating the effort required, it is the number of instructions per hour

TASK	%	EFFORT (MAN WEEKS)
PROBLEM ANALYSIS	8.2	11.2
PROJECT PLANNING	5.7	7.8
HARDWARE DESIGN	12.1	16.5
SOFTWARE DESIGN	12.6	17.1
PROGRAMMING	10.9	14.8
HARDWARE TESTING	19.8	26.9
SOFTWARE TESTING	13.8	18.7
PROTOTYPE EVALUATION	9.1	12.4
DOCUMENTATION	7.8	10.6
	100.0	136.0

FIG. 5.5-1 BREAKDOWN OF EFFORT FOR MICROPROCESSOR SYSTEM DEVELOPMENT. (AVERAGE FIGURES TAKEN FROM ERA SURVEY OF USERS)

which is important and using an 8 bit microprocessor one instruction is typically equivalent to between 2 and 2½ bytes. Thus, on 8 bit microprocessors, a programming rate of about 0.8 instruction per hour seems to be typical. Four bit microprocessors require about 1½ bytes per instruction while 16 bit microprocessors require between 2 bytes (e.g., Miproc) and about 4 bytes (e.g. LSI 11).

These figures may appear very low, but are not in fact too far removed from experiences in minicomputer programming, bearing in mind the lower level of support on microcomputers, the general lack of expertise in this new field and the additional system problems usually encountered.

It is, for example, generally accepted on larger machines that experienced programmers produce between 1 and 5 instructions per hour, or in the case of high level languages between 1 and 5 statements per hour. (The programming language does not appear to be relevant.)

Thus if the program size can be estimated, the effort required to implement it can also be estimated, and progress checked against the breakdown in Fig.5.5-1.

One of the ways to estimate the program size, if a hardwired logic version of the system exists as is sometimes the case, is to use the figure of 1 to 2 bytes as being equivalent to 1 hardwired gate. Thus if a circuit containing N gates is to be implemented in software, typically between N and 2N bytes of program will be needed. Obviously, such an equivalence is highly dependent on the type of microprocessor used, the type of application etc., so it should be used only as a rough guide when no other estimates are available.

A more reliable way to estimate the program size is to break it down into its component parts and add up the individual estimates for the various parts. Communication between these parts, general overheads and unforeseen problems are likely to result in the need to double these initial estimates. Those readers who feel somewhat inadequately prepared for this software estimating exercise may take comfort in the fact that they are not alone; even experienced software houses have been known to exceed their original estimates by more than thirty times! In such cases, the excess is often partially due to drastic specification changes. In fact, one of the comments noted many times in the questionnaire replies was that in future projects greater effort would be spent on preparing the specification before starting work on the software.

5.6 Project staffing

In considering the staffing of a project it is essential that the project objectives are clearly established since these can range from a simple desire to gain experience, right through to the necessity of getting a new product on the market in the shortest possible time.

Although the desire for experience and willingness to invest money for that purpose is surprisingly common and not confined to the large company alone, we shall not take it as a relevant objective since the attitude to timescale and expenditure is likely to be very different — in fact it may well become a part time operation.

If we assume therefore that we are dealing with a real project its objectives can range from the development of a prototype for market evaluation to the already mentioned need to hit the market at the right time with a fully developed product. In the former case, control of the development cost and the achievement or proving of technical performance, are likely to take precedence over timescales. In the latter, meeting timescale, specification and product cost targets will be more important than development expenditure.

These factors have a considerable bearing on the decisions made and the approach taken in regard to staffing the project.

5.6.1 Team size and structures

An early and important decision to be made is the size of team needed, since this is not purely dependent upon the size of the project. In this field especially in regard to software development 'small is beautiful' and the tendency to put in a large team to get the job done should be resisted — particularly later on if the project gets behind schedule.

Synergy is conspicuous by its absence in this type of work and the larger the team the less efficient it will become, since there is then a greater need for more communication just to keep everyone in step and in the software testing stage severe bottlenecks can develop unless several software testing facilities are available. Nevertheless, on the large project an acceptable timescale will force the acceptance of some inefficiency while on the small project it is probably a good idea to have a minimum project team slightly larger than that dictated by the work content.

There are two good reasons for this:

- If the team is too small it can get by with inadequate documentation and rely too heavily on personal contact and verbal communication. Sooner or later this causes problems which most often emerge later on in the systems integration and test phase when their correction is most costly.

- It is always desirable to have more than one man for each function just in case he falls ill or leaves. Continuity is an important and underrated factor in project control largely because its cost effect can seldom be measured since there is no 'control project' to provide a comparison.

As a result a minimum project team size is probably three, ideally comprising:

- a systems engineer with hardware and software experience

- a software specialist or programmer

- a hardware specialist

The systems engineer, who need not be full time, should normally have the most experience and be capable of doing the jobs of either of the other two, rather than being the man with the least experience, not capable of doing either job, as is more common. This also provides each of the other members of the team with a discussion partner, which is essential if potential solutions to problems are going to be adequately examined. It also provides continuity in the event of one of the three leaving. Continuity of staff is extremely important on the software side, since it is virtually impossible for replacement staff to pick up a half finished program and complete it, unless the documentation is near perfect, which is rarely the case.

An alternative is to use staff with both hardware and software experience only, in which case the team size can be reduced to two people. This approach is adopted by many companies and is a satisfactory approach, if the two members of staff concerned really are good at both hardware and software design.

On larger projects which require more staff, it is necessary to divide up the tasks between members of the team. The best procedure, particularly in the software area, is for the more experienced staff to handle the overall planning and the design of the top level hardware blocks and main program parts, and for them to identify self-contained sub-sections which can be delegated to more junior staff. In this way the interfacing between the various hardware and software modules is minimised. Note, however, that only an experienced designer can do this partitioning of the problem into sections properly.

5.6.2 Experience

In general finding staff with the necessary hardware expertise is not too difficult and few companies embark on this type of development without either some in-house electronics staff or the recruitment of a key man with this experience. A good starting point for microprocessor system hardware design is a thorough knowledge of modern logic design with integrated circuits. Most engineers nowadays have some knowledge of digital logic design so that competent designers in this field are not difficult to find. As microprocessors themselves evolve, they are becoming easier to use, particularly when supported by a good range of peripheral chips. The design of the hardware is thus becoming more and more straightforward.

What is often lacking and harder to obtain are staff with the necessary experience and training in system and software design. The intangibility and deceptive flexibility of software is something that engineers have been stumbling over since the transistor unleashed the automation revolution.

It is in fact vital that the project team contains at least one person with experience of system design in small real time computer systems or in the microprocessor field. There is in this area no substitute for experience and if no one is available in-house, on the job learning could be an expensive policy.

A background of minicomputer programming is an ideal starting point for microprocessor programming, but this should be based on experience of programming in assembler language, since microprocessors require an understanding of computer architectures if they are to be programmed effectively.   This cannot be obtained purely from working in a high level language such as Fortran.

5.6.3 Use of external services

External services, whether they come from other divisions of the company or from a specialist systems house, are a useful way of getting over a hump or providing time to train up one's own resources without the penalty of delaying the project. They must, however, be used without self-delusion and with very clear terms of reference, since it is never possible to sub-contract a problem, only the solution.

The two major advantages of external services are firstly that they provide (or should provide) an immediate injection of experienced staff in the vital areas of system and software design; secondly, they bring in a professional approach to organisation and documentation which is essential for the effective control of the project. If the service being considered does not measure up to these two points then it is not worth using.

On the reverse side of the coin there are some problems and disadvantages. The external staff will have to learn about the application and it is possible to fall into the trap of becoming overdependent upon them so that site problems prove difficult to solve.

However, if timescales have to be met, the use of external services is quite often the optimum way of ensuring success. The best way to ensure failure is to throw an inexperienced engineer into the deep end with loads of literature and conflicting advice in the hope that he will surface with the solution.

5.6.4 Training

The recent ERA survey showed that on average only 3.6 days per year were devoted to formal training.   In view of the complexity and newness of the subject, this low figure is indeed surprising.

The best form of training is on-the-job training. Ideally a trainee should join a team of experienced microprocessor engineers who spend a small amount of time, maybe two man weeks over a six month period, explaining

how everything works.   It is important to start at the beginning so
that fundamental principles are understood.   This means starting with
machine code and loading programs in through a front panel (difficult
nowadays with front panel-less equipment), graduating to assembler using
a paper tape system and finally to mass storage based operating systems.
The ERA survey showed that generally people were satisfied with whatever
courses they had attended, and therefore in the absence of a suitable
in-house environment the necessary training can be partially obtained
through manufacturers' and independent suppliers' courses.

SECTION 6

SETTING UP THE DEVELOPMENT LABORATORY

6.0 SETTING UP THE DEVELOPMENT LABORATORY

The development of a microprocessor based system requires the use
of a range of hardware and software support aids which are rather
different to those used for conventional hardware development. In
this section we outline the options open when establishing a development facility and the role of each of the support aids needed. As
the selection and comparison of specific development systems form
the major part of the later phases of the project, only general
details are included here.

6.1 The development process

In order to appreciate the role of each of the development tools
described, it is important to understand the problems facing the
designer and the way in which a system is developed.

6.1.1 Specifying the system

Ideally, the starting point is a specification of what the system
should do; in practice the specification is rarely finalised until
much of the work has already been performed, since microprocessors
offer so many opportunities to build in extras. The potential for
such enhancements is often only recognised when the design is well
under way. It is therefore important to explore as many avenues
as possible before committing the design to one direction and to
design in such a way that alterations are easy to implement. There
are many techniques available to improve the quality, flexibility
and reliability of software and the use of such techniques often
involves using the computer to perform some of the more mechanical
aspects of software design, which in turn implies a greater depen-
dence on the software tools employed.

6.1.2 Hardware/software design

At an early stage in the design process, the problem is divided into
two sections. One section is implemented in hardware, the other in
software. A comparison of the different steps involved is shown in
Fig. 6.1.2-1. The decision on how this division should be made
involves a trade-off between hardware and software.

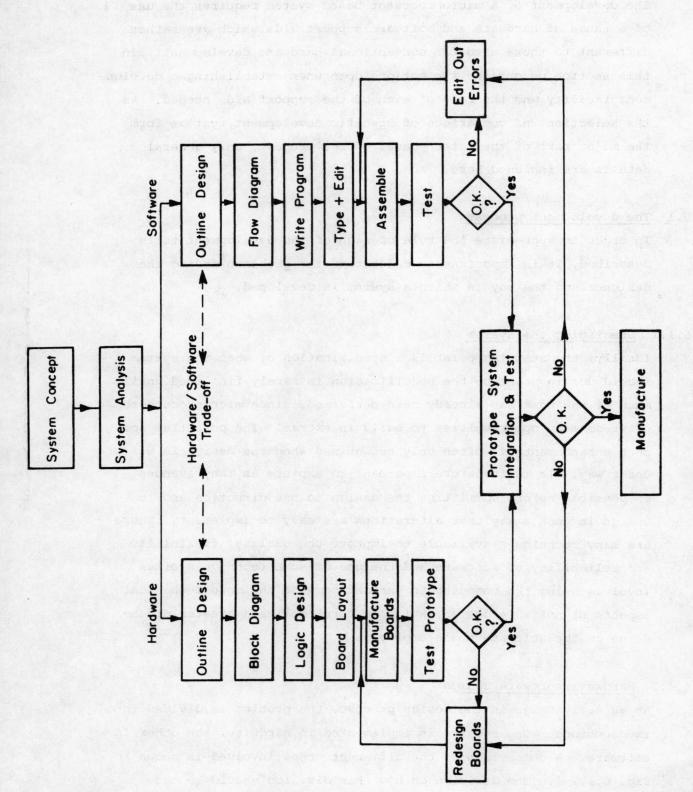

FIG. 6·1·2—1 TYPICAL DEVELOPMENT PROCESS.

As an example, a digital counting function could either be implemented using standard integrated circuits or by using counting
(increment) instructions in the program. The exact choice will
depend on various factors such as the loading on the microprocessor,
the counting speed required,etc.. At this stage the choice of microprocessor must also be made and then the detailed design can start.
In most cases, the design of the hardware is relatively straightforward since the leading microprocessor manufacturers now offer a
range of compatible integrated circuits which can simply be wired
together in a fixed manner in order to make a microcomputer. The
problem is of course different in more advanced applications which
involve a considerable amount of external hardware, but here standard
digital design methods and tools can be used.

6.1.3 Hardware testing

The greatest problem facing the hardware development engineer is
likely to be testing. In conventional hardware systems, the
functionality of a part of the system can usually be verified by
stimulating it in some way and then checking that the expected
response is obtained after a small delay. In the case of a microprocessor based system, testing the hardware is difficult without
the active cooperation of the microprocessor itself. In other words,
unless sufficient hardware is working to run small test programs,
fault diagnosis can be very difficult. Looking at it from another
point of view, once the central part is working, it can be used as
an aid to test the rest.

Development aids which monitor the behaviour of the microprocessor
system and trigger on complex combinations of events are now common-
place and greatly facilitate the testing process.

6.1.4 Programming

Programming can be reduced to creating patterns of ones and zeros
which are stored in a memory to control the microprocessor. The
direct generation of these patterns, known as programming in machine
code,is very tedious, very prone to errors and very inflexible. One
minor alteration near the beginning of such a machine code program
is likely to necessitate extensive modification of the subsequent
parts, something which can best be achieved by rewriting it completely.

Considerable improvements can be obtained by writing the program in
an assembly or a high level language. These concepts allow the
programmer to write in a kind of stylized English, using easily
remembered abbreviations to represent instructions and user defined
symbols to represent variables and constants. The translation from
either the assembly or the high level language is a mechanical process
which is normally done by an assembler or a compiler respectively.
These are themselves programs which have to run on some computer
which may or may not be based on the microprocessor in question.
Before either of these programs can be used, the original or source
program,as it is called,has to be prepared in a form which is
acceptable as an input to the assembler or compiler. It is usually
punched in a coded form onto paper tape or stored on a disc or
magnetic tape. To assist in the preparation of this source code an
editor is used. This is a program whose basic function is to accept
information typed in through a keyboard and to store it on paper
tape etc.. Facilities are also provided to correct typing errors and
to read in previously generated tapes in order to type in alterations.

Once the program has been prepared using the editor and translated
using an assembler or a compiler, a so-called object program is
obtained. This is equivalent to the machine code program mentioned
earlier and consists of a pattern of ones and zeros which must be
loaded into memory in order to test it. This is done using a loader
program which reads the tape and deposits the information in memory.

6.1.5 Program testing

There are various aids which can be used in the testing phase. Since
the concept of testing is well understood, the necessity for this
phase need not be expanded upon and the discussion of the tools
available for testing will therefore be left until later. After
testing it is usually necessary to go back and modify the source
program with the editor and to try again. This normally needs to be
done several times before everything works satisfactorily. It is
found in practice that even experienced programmers spend almost 50%
of their time in this testing and correcting cycle. The importance
of good aids, particularly in the testing phase therefore cannot be
stressed too much.

6.2 <u>Software development aids</u>

There are three basic software aids in use for the development of
microprocessor systems, namely the editor, the assembler and the
debugging routine. The editor is used to prepare the program onto
some storage medium such as paper tape, the assembler to translate
it into a form understandable by the microprocessor, and the debugging
routine to trace the errors. In addition many other types of aid
are used in order to speed up the development process.

6.2.1 <u>The "Editor"</u>

An editor is a program which reads a source program in (or in fact
any text such as a report) and allows the user to say via the teletype what he wants to have altered and how, and then to punch out a
corrected tape. In its simplest form it just allows the user to
type a line number, followed by what should be on that line. This
new line is then substituted for the original incorrect line.

Several lines can be corrected, usually in any order, and facilities
are always provided to print out any desired line by giving its
number. The user can thereby check that he is altering the right
line and also verify the correction. Since the editor must somehow
know when it gets a line number whether to print the line or change
it, more than just a line number must be given. For example, the
line number could be preceded (or followed) by a P for 'print' or a
C for 'change' as the case may be. These are called editor commands.

The editor described so far is still very unsophisticated. A good
editor should have the following additional features:

- The ability to delete a given line.
- The ability to insert new lines between two
  given lines.
- The ability to change the order of lines.
  For example a command to 'move lines 123
  through 157 to before line 27'.

- Since the whole of a source program may
  not fit into the computer at the same time,
  facilities should be provided to handle
  parts of programs. To do this the source
  program is often divided into segments by
  a special character (which the assembler
  ignores). These segments must be small
  enough to fit into the editor text buffer.
  In this case commands must be provided to
  read a segment in, punch a segment out
  and to clear the text buffer. Note that it
  is not possible for the move command to
  operate across a segment boundary.

- The ability to print out the whole text buffer.

- The ability in text mode to correct small
  typing errors, which are noticed immediately,
  by typing RUBOUT or some such special character.

- The ability to add fresh text to an empty
  or partly full buffer. This has two uses.
  Firstly, the obvious one of adding to existing
  programs, and secondly to prepare a program
  in the first place. Here the editor is used
  without an input tape, and a newly written
  program is typed straight into the editor, and
  typing errors can be corrected as they occur.

- The ability to search the text buffer for a
  given character string. This is an extremely
  useful command which avoids the necessity of
  knowing the line number on which an error
  occurs. For example, if the assembler gives
  out an error message of the form:

      US   STARQ   BEGIN + 7   406

  which means that the symbol STARQ was undefined,
  the user might recognise this as the word START
  with a typing error. The word START may occur
  hundreds of times in a program, and to find out
  which is wrong is tedious. Although the assembler
  should say where it occurred (BEGIN + 7), not all
  assemblers do. The user simply loads the editor,
  reads his program in and gives the commands:

      S   "STARQ"   (Search for STARQ)
      *P   (print whatever line it is on)
      JMP STARQ   (reply from editor)
      *C   (change whatever line it is on)
      JMP START   (corrected line typed)

The symbol * is equivalent to the current line
number. It is a shorthand way of referring to a
line without needing to know the numerical
value of the line number.

- The ability to change parts of a line so
that the whole line does not have to be
retyped. To do this, facilities are needed
to search a given line for a given character,
make an alteration either forwards or backwards, and then get the computer to complete
the line.

All the above features should be available on a good basic editor,
with various obvious simple extensions such as the ability to print
lines X to Y with one command. More advanced editors may have other
features as follows:

- The ability to work with other peripherals
such as high speed readers and punches,
alphanumeric displays etc.
- The ability to search over segment boundaries.
- The ability to search-and-replace, ie. to
replace all occurrences of a given text string
in a program by another text string.

Editors vary considerably in the facilities they offer and in the
way they are used. There are for example editors intended for use
with an alphanumeric display which make heavy use of a movable cursor,
and others which are letter rather than line orientated. The above
description should be taken therefore only as an example.

6.2.2 The "Assembler"

When the source program (See Fig. 6.2.2-1) has been prepared with
the editor, it is translated into the object program using an
assembler.

There are four main functions which an assembler has to perform,
and it has to read the source program tape at least twice to do
these functions. These functions are to translate the mnemonics
which represent the instructions into binary, to assign memory
locations to user symbols, to generate an object tape and to print
out a listing.

The first of these appears relatively straightforward. The assembler
contains a table of all instructions with their binary equivalents,
and translation simply involves reading in the program line by line
and looking up the required binary and punching it.

```
; PRØGRAM TITLE :-   16 X 16 BIT MULTIPLY RØUTINE
;
;  PERFØRMS (DE) = (BC) X (HL)


MPY16:    SHLD     TEMP     ; MULTIPLICAND TØ TEMP. STØRE
          LXI      H,BNUM   ; STØRE
          MVI      M,11H    ;  BIT CØUNT
          LXI      D,0      ; INITIALISE RESULT


LØØP:     MØV      A,B      ; RØTATE
          RAR               ;  MULTIPLIER
          MØV      B,A      ;   ØNE
          MØV      A,C      ;    BIT
          RAR               ;     RIGHT
          MØV      C,A
          DCR      M        ; DECREMENT BIT CØUNT
          RZ                ; RETURN IF LAST BIT

          JNC      NØADD    ; JUMP IF NØ CARRY
          LHLD     TEMP     ; ELSE ADD
          DAD      D        ;  MULTIPLICAND
          XCHG              ; SAVE TEMP. RESULT
          LXI      H,BNUM   ; RESTØRE (HL)

NØADD:    MØV      A,D      ; RØTATE
          RAR               ;  TEMP.
          MØV      D,A      ;   RESULT
          MØV      A,E      ;    ØNE
          RAR               ;     BIT
          MØV      E,A      ;      RIGHT
          JMP      LØØP     ; REPEAT

TEMP:     DS       2
BNUM:     DS       1

          END
```

Fig.6.2.2-1: Example of source program in Intel 8080 Assembler

For example, the instruction HLT might have a binary equivalent of
0lll0ll0. The instruction JMP START contains a user defined symbol:
START. This symbol must be defined somewhere in the program as otherwise it cannot be translated. The instruction tells the microprocessor to jump to the address START. This could involve jumping
backwards or forwards. If the jump is forwards, the address will
not have been defined at the time the translation is attempted
because its definition will not yet have been reached.

The phase in which the translation is done and an object tape
generated must therefore be preceeded by a kind of "trial run" in
which all the user symbols are sought out, and their numerical
equivalents ascertained and tabulated. This is known as the first
pass (through the reader). In order to do this the source tape is
read and the user symbol table generated (Fig. 6.2.2-3). The source
tape is then read a second time, during which the actual translation
is done, and the object tape produced (the second pass).

The listing (Fig. 6.2.2 -2) is a copy of the source program to which
two columns of figures have been added on the left. The first column
contains the numerical addresses where the instructions are to be
stored in memory, and the second the numerical equivalents of the
instructions. They are usually in hexadecimal or octal. For example
the instruction HLT might appear as 512 76 HLT, where 512 is the
address and 76 the value of HLT. The listing is a very important
piece of documentation which is essential during the debugging and
testing phase. It is normally printed by the assembler either
at the same time as the object tape is generated or afterwards.
When the assembler uses the teletype punch to produce the object
program it cannot print the listing on the teletype at the same time
and a third pass is therefore required for the listing.

The assembler is referred to as a two or three pass assembler
accordingly. Single pass assemblers also exist. Here the source
program is read into memory once and the assembler then scans it
for the symbols as it needs them. This is much faster than reading
it in twice but is only applicable to small programs or computers
with large memories where the source program fits into memory along
with the assembler.

```
                    ; PRØGRAM TITLE :-   16 X 16 BIT MULTIPLY RØUTINE
                    ;
                    ;  PERFØRMS (DE) = (BC) X (HL)


0000 222700  MPY16:  SHLD    TEMP    ; MULTIPLICAND TØ TEMP. STØRE
0003 212900          LXI     H, BNUM ; STØRE
0006 3611            MVI     M, 11H  ;  BIT CØUNT
0008 110000          LXI     D, 0    ; INITIALISE RESULT

000B 78      LØØP:   MØV     A, B    ; RØTATE
000C 1F              RAR             ;  MULTIPLIER
000D 47              MØV     B, A    ;   ØNE
000E 79              MØV     A, C    ;    BIT
000F 1F              RAR             ;     RIGHT
0010 4F              MØV     C, A    ;
0011 35              DCR     M       ; DECREMENT BIT CØUNT
0012 C8              RZ              ; RETURN IF LAST BIT

0013 D21E00          JNC     NØADD   ; JUMP IF NØ CARRY
0016 2A2700          LHLD    TEMP    ; ELSE ADD
0019 19              DAD     D       ;  MULTIPLICAND
001A EB              XCHG            ; SAVE TEMP. RESULT
001B 212900          LXI     H, BNUM ; RESTØRE (HL)

001E 7A      NØADD:  MØV     A, D    ; RØTATE
001F 1F              RAR             ;  TEMP.
0020 57              MØV     D, A    ;   RESULT
0021 7B              MØV     A, E    ;    ØNE
0022 1F              RAR             ;     BIT
0023 5F              MØV     E, A    ;      RIGHT
0024 C30B00          JMP     LØØP    ; REPEAT

0027         TEMP:   DS      2
0029         BNUM:   DS      1

                     END
```

Fig.6.2.2-2: Listing of the source program in Fig.6.2.2-1

```
BNUM  0029     LØØP  000B     MPY16 0000     NØADD 001E
TEMP  0027
```

Fig.6.2.2-3: Symbol table for listing in Fig.6.2.2-2

Alternatively, the symbols are left blank and filled in when the object program is loaded into memory by a linking loader. It should be noted here that a source program requires at least an order of magnitude more memory space than the object program.

6.2.3 Assembly errors

Apart from actual logical errors made at the time of conceiving a program, a programmer can make various other mistakes. If for example he writes the instruction JMP START and then forgets to define START (for example by not writing it as an address followed by a colon), the assembler will not be able to assemble this instruction. It should indicate this with an error message, ideally of the form:

US   START   BEGIN + 2   406

Here, US indicates the type of error, ie. undefined symbol, START is the undefined symbol, and BEGIN + 2 and 406 are where it occured. Unfortunately, few assemblers print out so much information, all of which is useful in a large program. The type of error must be printed so that the programmer knows what is wrong and the undefined symbol should be printed because the programmer might recognize it; he might have mistyped it as STARQ for example. With the help of a good editor program he can correct such errors without knowing where they are. It is important to type the actual address so that it can be found quickly in the listing, and it is important to type the address relative to the nearest symbolic address in case the programmer wishes to correct it without bothering to wait for a listing. There is nothing more frustrating than an error message of the form:

ERROR   406

Typical types of errors which can occur are:

- Undefined symbol
- Symbol defined twice
- Illegal addressing mode
- Illegal use of directive   eg. JNZ ORG

- Symbol table full
- Illegal character   eg. MOV %, A
- Illegal hexadecimal number   eg. 1974G
- END etc. missing
- Too many/few operands   eg. MOV A, B, C
- Integer too large   eg. 175452834

6.2.4. Advanced assembler features

As well as the basic assembler features discussed so far, most assemblers have extra features to ease program writing. For example, if a programmer wishes to reserve a block of memory full of zeros for a table 100 locations long, it is tedious to write 0 a hundred times. Some assemblers have a directive of the form:

ZERO 100

which does the function automatically.

Other typical features are:

- The ability to choose the radix of the numbers in the program with directives of the form OCTAL, DECIMAL etc.

- The ability to evaluate Boolean and mathematical expressions.

- Conditional assembly if specified Boolean expressions are true.

- Automatic address mode selection. Here the assembler chooses the addressing mode most suited to the circumstances, usually on the basis of minimum memory requirements. It is essential to be able to override this facility since in some situations it produces undesirable results. Such assemblers do exist without an override facility and they should be avoided.

- Text string facilities to translate text into the equivalent ASCII characters and place them in successive memory locations.

- Macro facilities. A macro is a shorthand way of including a string of instructions into a program. For example, the macro MULT might be defined as being equivalent to a sequence of say ten instructions which multiply two numbers together. Instead of writing out these ten instructions each time a multiply is required it suffices to write MULT. This is then recognised and the appropriate ten instructions substituted.

6.2.5 Debugging routines

When a person has written a program, assembled it, edited out all
the errors noticed by the assembler and reassembled it, it is still
very likely to contain errors. These errors are only noticed when
the programmer loads his program into memory using the binary loader,
and finds that it does not work as expected due to errors in the
algorithm or its implementation. Typical implementation errors are
forgetting to clear a register before using it, testing flags for
the wrong state, using the wrong addressing mode, calling a subroutine with a JMP instead of a CALL and forgetting that certain
instructions influence information stored in the flags etc.

All these types of errors are best found by going through the
program in slow motion with the aid of a so-called debugging routine.
This allows the user to break his program down into small manageable
sized parts which can be tested separately. It enables him to
examine intermediate results, simulate other intermediate results to
test the next section, and to make minor program modifications without the need for an assembler. These modifications should be
regarded as a temporary measure just for test purposes. After the
error has been found, the source program should be edited and reassembled so that an up-to-date listing is produced.

To use a debugging routine, it is loaded into memory with the user's
program. The memory must of course be large enough to hold both
simultaneously. The basic facility of a debugging routine is to
allow the user to type an address on the teletype, followed by some
special character, which causes the debugging routine to reply
with the contents of that address. This allows the user to check
intermediate results in memory, and to verify that his program is
still there. (It might not be, since errors can cause larger
sections to be overwritten.) If the programmer is satisfied with
the contents of the location printed out, he can type another
special character to indicate to the debugging routine that he has
finished with this address, or he can change its contents. Thus he
can modify the program or simulate intermediate results.

Some more sophisticated debugging routines have a simple assembler incorporated in them so that the user can talk to it using mnemonics instead of numbers. If it is only a numerical debugging routine, the user must do his own conversions to and from assembly language.

6.2.6 Breakpoints

In order to test a program in sections most debugging routines have a breakpoint facility. Assume that the user wishes to test the first part of his program, up to address N. He types a command to insert a breakpoint at location N + 1 (eg. command could be 1234 B). The debugging routine then swaps the instruction in this location for a jump to a special routine within itself, called the break-point routine. The original instruction is saved somewhere in a temporary location. The user then gives another command which tells the debugging routine to start the user program (eg. S 200 for start at 200). Control is thus transferred to the user program and the debugging routine becomes inoperative.

Several things can now happen. The user program can be so bad that it destroys the debugging routine, in which case the user has to load everything into memory again and start from scratch with a smaller value of N. The second possibility is that the user's program comes to a program halt or enters a never ending loop. In this case the debugging routine is not destroyed, and it is sufficient to start again with a smaller value of N.

The third possibility is that the program reaches location N + 1. (The program part just run may still contain errors). Since location N + 1 contains a jump to the breakpoint routine, control is trans-ferred back to the debugging routine, which immediately stores the values of all active registers and flags and also prints them out so that the programmer can check that they are as expected. The programmer can then examine other intermediate results stored in memory by typing their addresses as before. If the programmer is satisfied that that part of the program is working, he moves the breakpoint forwards to another location and continues with the testing.

To test the next part, the programmer gives a command to continue.
The debugging routine then replaces all active registers and flags
and jumps to location N + 1. Note that it should not be necessary
to start the program again from the beginning. This is important,
because it allows the user to modify the results of the first part
in order to test the second part more effectively. In this manner,
errors can be quickly located and corrected. Note also that a
breakpoint should not be placed on a sub-routine argument or on the
second or third words of a multiword instruction.

6.2.7 High level languages

Instead of writing programs in assembler the user may decide to use
a high level language like PL/M, Coral 66 or Fortran. While an
assembly language has almost a one to one relationship with the
machine code and is hence fixed for a given computer, in theory a
high level language is machine independent. Thus each program
statement is converted by a compiler into a series of machine code
statements to execute that particular command so that the compiler
rather than the language is peculiar to the machine.

In microprocessor applications the advantages of high level
languages, flexibility, machine independence, short programming time
etc. are offset by the increased memory required, problems of testing
and the need for larger support systems to run the compiler. In
general, assembler is more effective where the product unit cost and
performance are more important than the development timescale.
It is mainly on the low volume or one off prototype development
against a tight schedule that use of a high level language will
prove worthwhile.

6.2.8 Binary loaders

When the object tape has been produced, either by the assembler or
high level language compiler, the program can be loaded into memory.
A binary loader is used for this purpose. The object tape contains
addresses and data in binary, and the data is simply put into the
locations specified by the addresses. Normally some sort of parity
check is included since the data does not contain redundancies
as in the case of a source program.

A binary loader is of course not necessary if the program is put
straight into PROM's using a PROM loader (See 6.4.2.6). Note
however, that the PROM loader equipment itself contains a binary
loader.

6.2.9 Utility routines and subroutines

This heading covers all the little programs written to perform
functions such as calculations of mathematical functions (sines,
cosines, logarithms, integrals etc. up to fast fourier transforms,
(FFT's) and other routines which help the user run his system, for
example programs to print the contents of memory in octal or hexadecimal (memory dump programs) and to load PROM's from paper tape.
Many of these are written by users of the computers who then offer
them to the manufacturer who distributes them to other potential
users. Some manufacturers organise a Users' Group with a program
library containing such programs. These programs are usually of
very diverse quality, but there are often several excellent programs
amongst the many versions of binary loaders and memory dump programs
that get submitted.

6.2.10 Simulators and emulators

A simulator is a program run on a medium or large computer which
interprets the microprocessor program instructions and simulates
the execution of them. Its advantage lies in its ability to
display every detail of the program execution and to allow testing
and program debugging before it is run on a microprocessor at all.
Many useful functions can be built into a simulator, such as program
traps, breakpoints, trace facilities, and memory protection. An
emulator performs a similar function but is more hardware based
and is constructed from an array of conventional (TTL) logic elements.

One of the main difficulties in using simulators is in handling the
input/output operations. A simulator does not normally work as fast
as the real microprocessor and therefore cannot be used in real time
applications. Attaching peripherals to a simulator is in any case
difficult, and so simulators are normally only used for testing
the computational part of programs. They are usually used when the
hardware being developed is not yet available. Emulators do not
suffer from this disadvantage.

6.2.11 <u>Operating systems</u>

An operating system is a program whose function is to handle the day-to-day running of the computer system. With most stand alone micro-processor systems these are fairly rudimentary and much of the comment below refers to larger computers used for software development (See Section 6.4.7). In order to permit this, programs and data are stored in files, which are just storage areas with a name, on a disc etc. On each disc or magnetic tape, etc., a directory exists which tells the operating system where each program is. To load a program, the operating system looks up its name in the directory, finds out where it is, how long it is, where it is to be put in memory, any other relevant data and then loads it. When told to store a program on a disc etc., it finds out from the directory where a space is available, stores the program and updates the directory.

There are various types of operating systems. The simplest just allows the user to give commands such as RUN ASSEMBLER, which causes the operating system to do so. The assembler then gets the operating system to ask for the names of the source program, and the names of the object file and listing. Normally the name of a peripheral device can also be given with each file so that the files can be kept where the user wants them. When the assembler has finished, it transfers control back to the operating system (sometimes called the monitor) which waits for the user to type the next command.

Foreground-background operating systems utilize this waiting time to run a low priority program so that the computer is used to its full extent. When another command comes, this background program is interrupted and the new foreground program started. Whenever there is a pause, ie. at the end of the program or whilst waiting for a peripheral, the background program is allowed to continue. The computer is thus never idle.

This can be extended to so-called time sharing systems in which many users sit at their own teletype, and the computer operating system runs each of their programs on a sort of flexible time-multiplexing scheme.

This works very well for jobs like editing or testing since the users spend most of the time thinking what to do next. It is sufficient to get a response from the teletype to a typed character within a hundred milliseconds or so as each user will hardly notice that the computer is not dedicated to his terminal alone.

Another type of operating system is the so-called batch-processing system. Here the operating system receives a list of programs to be run, and it runs one after the other with the minimum amount of time wasted in between. Most such systems are combined with a fore-ground-background system.

6.2.12 Monitors

The functions of a monitor are somewhat hard to define, since they vary so much from case to case. Debugging routines and operating systems are sometimes referred to as monitors, although the term usually refers to a minimal system containing a binary loader and some debugging facilities in order to assist the user to load and start other programs.

6.3 Basic support software requirements

In conclusion, there are several support programs which are essential if reasonable progress is to be made:

> (a) A good editor is necessary. It should have facilities for reading and punching paper tape, inserting, deleting and rearranging the order of text. Other facilities such as the ability to search text automatically for character strings and to change parts of lines without retyping the whole line are also very convenient. Since an editor can be used to edit any type of text, the editor of another computer can be used. For example, if a mini-computer is available, it could be used for editing programs for a microcomputer.

(b) An assembler is necessary. This can be a cross-assembler which runs on another computer, or a resident assembler which runs on the same computer. Macro facilities are useful but not essential. The assembler should produce a listing and a binary output suitable for loading into either RAM or PROMs via the PROM loader equipment.

(c) A debugging routine is necessary. This should provide facilities for examining and altering memory locations, searching memory for locations containing specific numbers, and setting and removing breakpoints. The ability to search memory for locations which do not contain a specified number and to search for parts of numbers is also very useful.

(d) Some means of loading programs from paper tape into memory and punching the contents of memory out onto paper tape is also necessary. These programs are fairly simple and can be written by the user. These should be stored in ROM. The other programs can be kept on paper tape or stored in ROMs. These ROMs are then plugged in when needed.

6.4 Hardware development aids

Hardware development aids are used as tools in the development of microprocessor systems and in conjunction with appropriate software aids can be used for several purposes:

1. As a teaching aid to familiarise staff with microprocessors.

2. As a host computer to develop microprocessor software.

3. As a debugging aid in fault finding.

Some hardware development aids cover all three of the above and others are aimed at specific ones. The different types of aid will be described in turn and the application areas covered by each one identified.

6.4.1 Introductory starter kits

Introductory starter kits are available from a variety of manufacturers for a few hundred pounds. They usually consist of a microprocessor with its associated clock driver and buffers etc. and between ¼K and 2K bytes of RAM, a small monitor-debugging program in ROM and a few bytes of input-output.

Some provide a hexadecimal keyboard and seven segment display, a 20 m.a. current loop interface for a teletype etc. and provision for user ROM's.

On their own they are not really much use as they do not provide enough facilities to enable the user to develop or test software economically and reliably. In addition, they are not particularly suited to training since the principles of operation of the micro-processor are masked by the implementation details and the com-promises inherent in the low cost board. In fact there is a danger that the novice user will start his microprocessor life in the wrong direction and never appreciate the need for a more orderly approach to microprocessor system design with the use of the correct tools, (ignorance is bliss). Some of the introductory kits can be extended. This is however, usually only possible in a limited fashion because many of the important signals on the board are not brought out to edge connection and because the address lines for both memory and input-output are not normally fully decoded.

6.4.2 Microprocessor development systems

A microprocessor development system is a stand alone computer based on a microprocessor. It consists of a cabinet with power supplies, slots for different types of boards and a certain amount of minimum hardware to enable it to function as a computer. Prices range from about £1500 for units intended for the hobbyist market up to about £5000 for the more expensive basic systems. These prices are, however, misleading. A typical system will usually need additional input-output boards and memory and will require at least a terminal with paper tape facilities before it can be used. A reasonably effective economy system will cost at least £8000 but if floppy discs and other more sophisticated peripherals are added, then the price rapidly reaches double that amount.

6.4.2.1 A good basic system

The question therefore arises as to what is needed to support a development laboratory. To answer this, it is necessary to consider the environment in which the unit is to work.

When the system is only for use by one or two engineers, who do not
work full time in this field, then a good basic system for around
£8000 will be found sufficient (See Fig. 6.4.2.1-1). This implies
that programs will be written in assembler using paper tape as the
storage medium. The fact that this involves longer development
times is offset by the savings in capital in going for the basic system.

6.4.2.2 High speed paper tape reader and punch

It is, however, worth acquiring a high speed paper tape reader and
punch, otherwise the loading and punching of programs can take
several hours which not only wastes time, but more important it
encourages the engineers to take short cuts. As an example of this,
an engineer might correct a fault in the object program instead of
editing and reassembling. Such an action is roughly equivalent to
modifying printed circuit boards by cutting tracks under integrated
circuits instead of having new boards made. Such actions are fine
as a temporary fix, but create havoc with the documentation, and if
practised frequently on one program can lead to the state where no
one knows how the program works.

6.4.2.3 In-circuit-emulators

Another option well worth having, when available, is some form of
in-circuit-emulation. (This phrase comes from the inventors, Intel,
but equivalents are available from other manufacturers under different
names.) It is used in the software and hardware debugging phases.
To use it, the microprocessor in the user's prototype is replaced by
a plug with a cable which goes into the development system.

Circuitry and software in the development system monitor what
happens in the user's prototype whilst it works with a remote processor,
situated in the development system. The user can thereby see what
is happening and make minor modifications to the program via the
terminal, without having to attach extra hardware to his prototype.
The in-circuit-emulation hardware allows the user to run his program
in parts, to use facilities in the microprocessor development
system and to access all the resources of the prototype hardware.

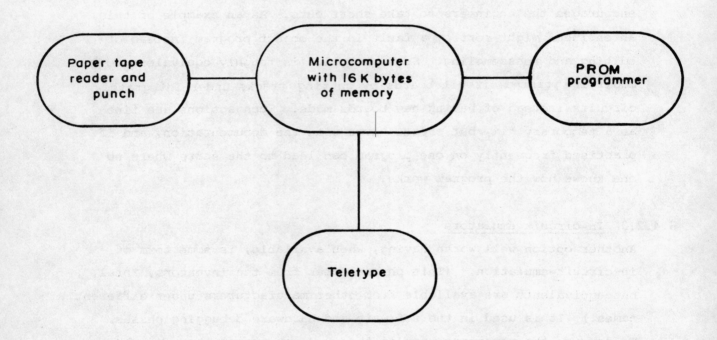

FIG. 6·4·2·1-1   A BASIC MICROPROCESSOR DEVELOPMENT SYSTEM.

6.4.2.4 Additional memory and backing storage

If the microprocessor development system is to be used rather more
heavily, then more memory and further peripherals are justified.
More memory is required if high level languages are to be used
because high level language compilers usually require considerable
amounts of memory.

The amount of memory required depends on the types of programs to
be run. It is technically quite possible to accommodate a reasonably
good assembler (See 6.2.2) in 4K bytes. 8K bytes of memory should
be ample to hold the assembler and provide enough room for the user's
symbol table. Unfortunately, many of the microprocessor manufacturers
do not offer reasonably good assemblers. They usually require
considerably more storage than is really necessary (they are sometimes written in a high level language) and they offer many features
which are only applicable to the more advanced users.

For this reason, the minimum amount of memory which is required is
often 16K bytes. A floppy disc based system which greatly speeds
up the loading and storing of programs often requires even more;
the Intel ISIS 2 disc based operating system for example will just
about run in 32K, and really needs 48K to work comfortably. Unfortunately, microprocessor software seems to have got a bit out of
control; there is nothing 'micro' about it any more. The recommended
minimum memory size is therefore usually governed by the requirements
of the support software rather than by the size of the user's program.
We shall be commenting on the requirements of the various microprocessor manufacturers' software packages in phase 3 of the project.

6.4.2.5 The effect of peripherals on load and edit times

The choice of extra peripherals like floppy discs is governed to a
great extent by the effect they can have on development time. For
example consider the times involved with a typical program about
4K bytes long.

As a general rule of thumb source tapes with an average amount of commenting require about ten times as many characters as the object tape ie. in our example 40,000 characters. In a teletype, working at 10 chr./sec., this would take over an hour to read in. If this contains a single error which is noticed during the second pass of the assembly process, the time wasted correcting it would typically be as follows:

1. Loading editor to correct it		15 mins.
2. Reading source into editor	1 hr.	6 mins.
3. Correcting error		negligible
4. Punching out corrected source	1 hr.	6 mins.
5. Reloading assembler		30 mins.
6. Repeating pass one of assembly	1 hr.	6 mins.
7. Repeating pass two of assembly	1 hr.	6 mins.
Total	5 hrs.	9 mins.

Using a high speed reader and punch, working at 200 chr./sec. and 100 chr./sec. respectively, this total is reduced to under 20 minutes.

With a floppy disc system the turn around time is no longer governed by the actual reading or writing speeds, but by the way in which the files are organised and the consequent amount of disc head movement required. Typically the time needed to correct the error would be around 5 minutes.

Unless the programmers are very experienced, a typical 4K program, if it were not debugged as it was developed would possibly contain hundreds of errors, many of which admittedly could be corrected at one sitting. It is difficult to carry this analysis further without making dubious assumptions since the habits of the equipment users will be altered by the facilities available. Using a floppy disc based system, a 4K program might be assembled hundreds of times in the course of it's development. (If its easy and costs nothing, it's done after every minor modification.)

On a high speed paper tape system, the number of assemblies would be kept to a minimum - say ten times. On a low speed paper tape system, it is likely to be assembled only two or three times and patches will be added to the object tape to avoid having to re-assemble. Then after a bit the patches themselves are patched and any record of how the program works is totally lost, reliability drops dramatically, and errors take ten times as long to find since no documentation exists.

6.4.2.6 Use of a PROM programmer

Once the software has been developed on the microprocessor develop-ment system, and debugged using the in-circuit-emulator, it is usually desirable to load it onto PROM for field testing before having expensive masks made for ROM. For this purpose a PROM programmer is used. This is a peripheral to the microprocessor development system which will enable the user to transfer programs from a storage device (paper tape, disc or memory) to the PROM. The PROM can then be plugged into the user's prototype and if all is well, the prototype can then be sent out for field trials. If a mistake is discovered, certain types of PROM (FAMOS PROM's) can be erased with an ultra violet light source, and the process repeated. This is a very convenient facility, and a well equipped laboratory will have a PROM programmer and a U.V. eraser. It is also possible to send the paper tape object program to a distributor and have PROM's programmed for a few pounds. This is obviously very economical if the quantities are small but does introduce a time delay into the process. Since different types of PROM's require slightly different programming sequences, general PROM programmers cater for different PROM's through small plug-in cards, known as personality cards. These act as an interface to the PROM and provide the right sequences and voltages etc. for the particular PROM for which they were designed.

6.4.2.7 A more advanced development system

A more advanced system (See Fig. 6.4.2.7-1) based on floppy discs would not necessarily include everything in the economy system.

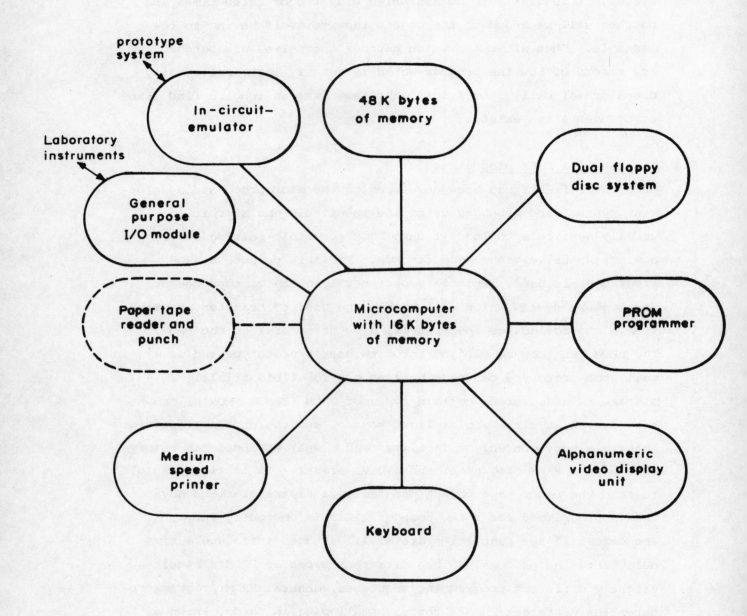

FIG. 6·4·2·7-1 AN ADVANCED MICROPROCESSOR DEVELOPMENT SYSTEM.

Firstly, the paper tape facilities could possibly be dispensed
with. They would however, be worth keeping if it were necessary
to be able to swap programs with other users. 8 channel paper tape
is such a universally accepted standard that paper tape facilities
are always useful as a means of interfacing with other people.

The second item which may not be present in an advanced system is
the teletype. To speed up the interaction with the development
system, the teletype can be replaced with an alphanumeric display
and keyboard. It is essential though to have some means of
obtaining a hard copy of programs and their listings. For this a
medium to high speed printer is required. Since microprocessor
development work is essentially interactive, (which is not the case
on large mainframe computers with batch operating systems) it should
not be necessary to have a high speed line printer. A dot matrix
printer working at a few tens of characters per second (eg. a DEC
writer) is usually adequate, and gives a fairly high quality hard
copy. A 30 chr./sec. printer will print a listing of a 4K byte
program with an average amount of commenting in about 45 minutes.
It is usually possible to arrange the working day so that the
development system does this listing during the lunch hour. There
is little point in having a very expensive line printer which prints
the listing in a few minutes, then stands idle for most of the day,
unless the system is used by a large team. Even then it might be
better to invest in a second development system with a medium speed
printer rather than buying a line printer. It is however easy to
see why teletypes are so popular. They provide, for a very low price,
a printer, a keyboard, a paper tape reader and a paper tape punch,
and although faster and more convenient peripherals are obtainable,
they are very expensive in comparison.

6.4.2.8 <u>Need for twin disc drives</u>

In a floppy disc based system it is important to have at least two
disc drives. A single disc drive does not enable the user to copy
from one disc to another which is essential. Copying can be done
with a single disc drive, using the memory as a buffer to hold a small
part of the disc information while the disc is swapped. This is,
however, very tedious and not recommended.

6.4.2.9 General purpose I/O interface

Another option which is likely to prove useful in both the economy
and advanced systems is a general purpose input-output interface.
It is useful for connecting non-standard peripherals or for
laboratory work as an interface to hardware under development. This
enables the user to test his own equipment and programs through
the development system using the sensors and actuators which will
later be part of the final prototype.

6.4.2.10 Availability of high level languages

It should be noted that most self-contained microprocessor development systems do not support high level language compilers. This
situation is likely to change over the next year or so, but it
should be borne in mind when deciding whether to opt for a stand
alone development system.

6.4.3 PROM simulators

A PROM simulator is basically a RAM with flying lead on the end of
which there is a plug. This plug is plugged into sockets where
ROM's normally reside, and the whole system acts like a ROM. When
the prototype into which it is plugged reads a location, the RAM
supplies the necessary information. The information is normally
loaded into the RAM via a small numerical keyboard associated with
the PROM simulator. This means that the user has to work in machine
code which is not likely to give good results on anything but the
smallest programs. What is really required is a connection to a
development system to allow programs to be developed using the normal
support software and then 'downloaded' into the PROM simulator. The
result is something similar to an in-circuit-emulator. Although it
is not quite as powerful, it does have one very large advantage: it
can be used for any type of microprocessor. Perhaps for this reason,
microprocessor manufacturers do not seem keen on supplying such
devices.

Extensions to the basic idea include personality cards to enable
different types of PROM or ROM to be simulated, and circuitry to
enable the system to simulate RAM chips also.

It is possible to obtain PROM simulators with batteries. These are
even more like a PROM in that they do not require power to retain
the information in them.

6.4.4 Logic analysers

Logic analysers are sometimes used for debugging microprocessor
based systems. They are used normally on digital systems in the same
way that oscilloscopes are used on analogue systems. Oscilloscopes
are not very suitable for debugging digital systems, particularly
microprocessor systems, because most digital systems have very
complex waveforms in which both the sequence of ones and zeros and
the time relationship between different waveforms is important.
Analysing such waveforms with an oscilloscope is very difficult,
particularly when the conditions of interest only appear very in-
frequently.

Logic analysers on the other hand are ideal for such work. A
logic analyser consists of a fast memory between 4 and 32 bits wide
and between 16 and 2048 words long. Information is gathered via
probes from the prototype under test and stored in the memory at
high speed one word after another.

It can then be displayed to the user, usually on a screen. The
clock which inputs the information to the memory can be either
internal (asynchronous) or derived from the prototype (synchronous).
Asynchronous analysers are usually used for debugging hardware with
a fast clock, so that glitches can be seen, whereas synchronous
analysers are more suitable for debugging software.

A triggering system similar to that found on an oscilloscope is
used to start the whole process, but unlike the oscilloscope trigger,
it can be combinatorial, in other words the trigger is only deemed
to have occured if a specified combination of events occur. The
display usually takes one of three forms. In the first the display
looks like a multibeam oscilloscope and will be familiar to all
designers. The only difference is that the display is likely to
contain considerably more beams than in a conventional oscilloscope,
and the waveforms will be idealised with no signs of ringing etc.

In the second display mode, referred to as a map, the data is
separated into two half words, each of which drives a digital to
analogue convertor, which deflects the X and Y beams of the
display. With a sixteen channel analyser, the display therefore
consists of a 2^{16} (65536) matrix, ie. 256 x 256 points which can be
either light or dark depending on whether the digital combination
occurred or not. It is possible with this type of display to see a
whole program working and identify whether the microprocessor is
executing parts of the program which should not be executed. A
movable cursor is often provided to assist in the identification of
particular points.

In the third display mode, the data pattern is shown as a sequence
of numbers in a selectable radix down the screen. This can be used
to show the machine code of a program which is running, as it runs.
Analysers are now becoming available with a disassembly feature
which display the microprocessor mnemonics rather than the machine
code. These contain personality cards which determine which microprocessors they can work with. The display then looks rather like
a listing.

As can be seen, logic analysers have evolved considerably in the
past few years, and new variations are emerging constantly.

6.4.5 Laboratory minicomputers

To use a minicomputer for microprocessor software development, at
least a cross-assembler or a cross-compiler is required. These are
sometimes available from the microprocessor supplier, or may be
written by the user (something which is not usually economical).
Most cross-software which can be purchased is written in Fortran, so
that it can be used on different types of host computer. If the
host computer is a minicomputer, it must therefore support Fortran
which usually requires a fairly large configuration. Since there
are also various dialects of Fortran, care should be taken before
purchasing cross-software in Fortran to make sure that it will run
on the particular type of minicomputer available. Occasionally,
cross-software is available in other languages such as Basic or assembler.

In order for a minicomputer to be attractive for microprocessor software development it should be equipped with a comprehensive range of peripherals. A suitable configuration will normally include a fairly large memory, a medium to high speed printer, discs, an alphanumeric display and a keyboard. Paper tape facilities are almost essential as a means of transferring the microprocessor programs between the minicomputer and microprocessor prototype or PROM programmer etc. Another option which might be preferable to paper tape is a direct link between the minicomputer and the microprocessor prototype. This is not difficult to make if the minicomputer has a general purpose digital input-output interface.

The advantages of using a laboratory minicomputer are that peripherals are usually more sophisticated which means that the turn around time is fast and it does not tie the user to any particular microprocessor manufacturer. It is also preferable to large company mainframes which tend to be too remote and inflexible. On the negative side, minicomputers require either a simulator for testing and debugging or some other support equipment such as a PROM simulator, logic analyser or low cost development system. A minicomputer is probably not the best choice for the occasional or small user, unless one is already available for other work. It is, however, often favoured by large users and software houses where the required flexibility justifies its cost, and where expertise exists to support it and get the most out of it.

It is worth noting that much of the minicomputer software can be used directly for microprocessor software development, in particular the editor, operating system and utilities for tape copying etc. These are often of a higher standard than microprocessor equivalents which is possibly another factor which could influence the choice.

6.4.6 <u>Commercial time sharing networks</u>

Commercial time sharing networks are another option available. They consist of large networks of computers, linked to each other and to users via communication channels.

Access to such networks can be obtained via the telephone system using a standard terminal and a Post Office modem (modulator-demodulator). In order to make use of such networks, the user telephones the nearest access point and after giving various code words and identification numbers via the terminal, can develop his programs on the remote computer. The fees vary between networks, but usually consist of several charges for different aspects of the service used (eg. central processor time, input-output channel time (connect time), characters transferred, discs used etc.). On top of this the cost of the telephone call must be added. This will depend on the location of the nearest access point, and can be quite high, since the call often lasts several hours.

The main attraction of the commercial time sharing networks is that the latest versions of the microprocessor support software from all the major manufacturers are accessable instantly. The low capital outlay is also very attractive, since a terminal can be obtained for as little as £1000. The modem has to be hired from the Post Office in the United Kingdom but other rules may apply abroad.

The disadvantage of the commercial time sharing networks is their very high recurrent cost. The cost of compiling a single high level language statement can often be about £1, although of course assembly will be much cheaper. This means that this approach should not be taken by heavy users, except when access to costly software is required. Time sharing networks are attractive for occasional users or those with a requirement to access many different manufacturer's software.

Like the minicomputer, this approach does not satisfy the complete development need. Although simulators are available, some form of hardware debugging capability such as a logic analyser is usually necessary.

6.4.7 In-house mainframe computers

Many companies have their own computer centres for commercial and scientific data processing.

Microprocessor software can be developed on these systems in one
of two ways: through batch processing and through local timesharing
terminals. In each case some form of hardware aid will be required
for testing the final prototype.

6.4.7.1 Batch processing

Batch processing is the classic data processing mode. A program
is submitted to the computer centre, where it joins a queue. The
computer processes each job in turn and there is no interaction
between the computer and the user. This makes it very difficult to
do certain types of work such as editing, and its remoteness makes
it unpopular with engineers. Like the minicomputer, cross-
software is required, but this is more likely to work straightaway,
because the larger size of the mainframe computer will support more
advanced Fortran operating systems. The turn around time tends to
be very slow compared to all the other on-line methods of software
development. The recurring costs can be fairly high, particularly
if simulation is used extensively, but in some cases the fact that
such a computer exists may mean that this is the preferred approach.
The cost of the cross-software should be borne in mind when making a
choice.

6.4.7.2 Local timesharing terminals

Many large computers support time sharing systems which enable a
local user to sit at his own terminal and interact with the computer.
Compared to batch processing this approach is more more amenable to
microprocessor software development. The main differences between
local timesharing and a commercial timesharing network are firstly
that the recurrent costs on local timesharing are much less, and
secondly that the required cross-software is not automatically available; it has to be purchased.

6.5 A comparison of the options

In the preceeding sections the range of software and hardware aids
available have been described in general terms and comments made upon
their suitability for various stages of system development.

Here general recommendations are made on the "package" required to equip a laboratory for development together with an indication of the costs. The existence of standard laboratory tools such as oscilloscopes and signal generators is assumed in each case.

6.5.1 The microprocessor development system approach

A microprocessor development system, unlike the other aids described, can provide all the facilities required for both hardware and software development. It is the most common approach for users dedicated to one type of microprocessor and even this limitation is beginning to be removed by the availability of universal prototyping systems such as the Tektronix 8002 which will be evaluated in Phases 2 and 3. As discussed earlier the capital investment required ranges from around £8000 for a basic but effective system to £16,000 for the advanced system required to ensure the best use of a development engineer's time. The two configurations are shown in Fig. 6.5.1-1. By contrast an equivalent universal advanced system would cost about £20,000 but would be equipped to handle two different microprocessors and with a capability to extend to others; clearly not an economic proposition for the laboratory firmly dedicated to one microprocessor but with attractions for those who need to keep their options open or serve a wide range of developments where different microprocessors may be necessary.

The above all assume the use of in-circuit-emulation for testing and debugging. As an alternative a logic analyser could be considered since it is a more general purpose development aid and can be used for a wide range of hardware and software related problems. Against this however, it is expensive, the typical equivalent products being £4000-£7000 compared with £600-£2000 for in-circuit-emulation.

6.5.2 The minicomputer approach

A good minicomputer with appropriate cross-software can form an excellent basis for a development laboratory. However, the capital cost of a minicomputer is between £6000 and £30,000, depending on the type and configuration.

BASIC SYSTEM CONFIGURATION

- Microcomputer with 16k bytes RAM
- Teletype
- Paper tape reader & punch
- PROM Programmer + 2 personality cards
- In-circuit-emulator

CAPITAL COST- ≈ £8,000

ADVANCED SYSTEM CONFIGURATION

- Microcomputer with 16k bytes RAM
- Alphanumeric display & keyboard
- Medium speed printer
- PROM Programmer + 2 personality cards
- In-circuit-emulator
- Extra 48k bytes RAM
- Dual floppy disc system
- General purpose I/O module
- Resident high level language compiler (if available)

CAPITAL COST- ≈ £16,000

FIG. 6·5·1—1 THE MICROPROCESSOR DEVELOPMENT SYSTEM APPROACH — ALTERNATIVE CONFIGURATIONS.

Cross-software is usually written in Fortran so that it can be run on a wide range of host computers, and this means that a powerful minicomputer, near the top end of the price bracket is required. The cross-software itself usually ranges in price from about £500 for a simple assembler to about £2,000 for an advanced compiler, with most macro-assemblers, simulators and basic compilers around £1000.

If a simulator is not used, the software can be tested on a cheap microprocessor based single board computer which costs typically £500, one of the introductory kits usually available for about £200, or on the prototype under construction if it is ready. In each case some form of terminal is required for operator inter- action. This could be a teletype costing about £1000.

The only remaining problem is transferring the programs to be tested from the minicomputer to the test environment. This can be done via a direct link to the minicomputer if a suitable digital input/output interface exists, or via paper tape; the minicomputer can punch a paper tape which is then read into the system via the teletype. This method is slow and not recommended. A fast paper tape reader solves this problem, but is not very elegant.

The programs can also be loaded into PROM's if a PROM programmer exists on the minicomputer. These can then be plugged into the test environment. Alternatively, a PROM simulator can be used. PROM simulators are however only of any real use in this situation if they can be loaded directly from the minicomputer. There is no point in having a PROM simulator which can only be loaded via a keyboard; one might just as well key the program into the test environment directly using the teletype. A simple PROM simulator costs about £400, but without a direct link capability or a high speed reader, they are not suitable for this type of work.

The minicomputer approach clearly appeals more to software specialists and is suitable for users with a variety of needs who wish to remain flexible.

The initial capital cost however is such that few users are likely
to pursue this path unless they already have a minicomputer or
access to one. The sort of department which is likely to have
such a minicomputer however, is likely to be software orientated.

6.5.3 The large computer approach

Timesharing and batch processing systems need to be augmented by a
hardware development and testing facility in the same way that the
minicomputer does. Unlike the minicomputer,however, it is usually
not possible to implement a direct link to the prototype under
construction.

A small microprocessor development system is sometimes used in
conjunction with a commercial time sharing network. Editing and
testing are then done locally, and the timesharing system used for
compilation and data storage. This combination provides good
facilities at a fairly low cost, and since the use of the timesharing system can be kept to a minimum, the recurring costs can be
kept under control. It is often possible to make the development
system behave like a terminal so that it can talk directly to the
timesharing network. If this is not done, transfers have to be done
via paper tape.

If a commercial timesharing system is used then this is undoubtedly
an expensive development approach requiring close control to avoid
wasteful use of the system.

Since the cost to any one user will be dependent upon their method
of working, the number of revisions, and the use of on line editing,
it is impractical to give a figure. A useful guideline however is
to regard the charges quoted as the tip of an iceberg.

Actual costs of using this type of service will be obtained in Phase
3 when this service is evaluated.

In spite of these comments, clearly the timesharing approach is very flexible and a valuable method of gaining experience before committing oneself to a particular microprocessor. It is also an effective way of pushing through a software development programme quickly since it removes the need for capital expenditure.

APPENDIX

GLOSSARY OF MICROELECTRONICS AND COMPUTER TERMS

APPENDIX

GLOSSARY OF MICROELECTRONICS AND COMPUTER TERMS

This glossary of terms has been produced by ERA as an aid to those being introduced to microelectronics for the first time. The definitions are therefore intended to be helpful rather than strictly formal. Unfortunately many manufacturers have adapted terms and standard words to suit there own products. The meanings therefore tend to vary from one manufacturer to another. This applies particularly to the various addressing modes commonly used. Care should be exercised therefore when the precise meaning is important.

A

ABORT - To deliberately discontinue an activity, in particular the execution of a computer program.

ABSOLUTE ADDRESS - A fixed address as opposed to one which may be altered or modified when a program using it is executed. Hence also ABSOLUTE LOCATION and ABSOLUTE PROGRAM.

ACCESS - The process of acquiring information from a computer register, memory or peripheral unit.

ACCESS TIME - The time which is taken to reference a particular item in storage, to read from or write to a memory location or a stored record on tape or disc.

ACCUMULATOR- A register in which numbers are totalled, manipulated, or temporarily stored for transfers to and from memory or external devices.

ADDER - A device which forms the sum of two binary numbers.

ADDRESS - (1) A unique label, name, or number that identifies a memory location or a device register for access by computer. (2) To send an address to a memory or device in order that a particular location in memory or the device may be identified.

ALGOL - Abbreviation for ALGOrithmic Language. A universal high level language especially suitable for writing programs of a mathematical nature.

ALGORITHM - A prescribed set of well-defined rules or processes, for the solution of a problem. Algorithms are implemented on a computer by a programmed sequence of instructions.

ALPHA-NUMERIC - Characters which may be letters of the alphabet or numerals.

ANALOG/ANALOGUE - The representation of numerical quantities by means of physical variables such as rotation, voltage or resistance or the representation of physical quantities by others more conveniently generated or measured.

ANALOG COMPUTER - (1) A computer in which analog representation of data is mainly used. (2) A computer that operates on analog data by performing physical processes on these data. Contrast with DIGITAL COMPUTER.

ANALOG REPRESENTATION - The representation of a variable by a physical quantity (such as angular position or voltage) which is made proportional to the variable.

ANALYST - A person who defines problems and develops algorithms and procedures for their solution.

AND - A logical operaton between two bits that results in a 1 if, and only if, both input bits are 1, and in 0 otherwise. The 'AND' operation between two multibit numbers is equivalent to the 'AND' operation between the corresponding bits of the two numbers.

APPLICATIONS PACKAGE - A specified combination of hardware and software which has been designed for a particular application. An applications package is not generally restricted to one configuration of plant or peripherals. It is usually assembled by the computer manufacturer or an independent supplier and sold as a complete system with the machine.

APPLICATIONS SOFTWARE - A suite of programs, written in any language, but unique in one application or configuration of plant and peripherals. It may be written by the manufacturer or the customer. It consists of the software written especially for a particular application of the computer.

ARCHITECTURE - The design of the internal physical structure of a system, and the way its components are interconnected.

ARCHIVE - To copy a tape, disc or other backing store media, so that in the event of one copy becoming unusable the original data is not lost.

ARGUMENT - (See Parameter) : A variable within a function. The function can only be evaluated when the value of the argument is defined. Subroutines (qv) and Macros (qv) often use one or more arguments.

ARITHMETICAL AND LOGICAL UNIT (ALU) - A device which executes arithmetic and/or logical operations according to the instructions in a program.

ARRAY - (See Matrix)

ASSEMBLER - A computer program which converts a symbolic assembly language program into an executable object (binary-coded) program. Depending on the assembler, the machine language program produced can be structured to occupy a set of absolute locations, or be movable (relocatable) to another set of locations in system memory by adding a given value (offset) to each assembled address.

ASSEMBLY LANGUAGE - A symbolic programming language which forms the input to an assembler. The assembly language itself cannot be used to operate the computer, it must first be assembled into the machine code.

ASYNCHRONOUS - A mode of operation in which the rate of data transmission between two devices is not related to any fixed frequency in the system.

AUTODECREMENT ADDRESSING - A method of addressing in which a constant, usually unity, is subtracted from an address immediately before or after the address is used to reference memory. It is used to access data stored as a list in sequential memory locations or in conjunction with AUTOINCREMENT ADDRESSING to form a PUSH DOWN LIST or STACK.

AUTOINCREMENT ADDRESSING - As in AUTODECREMENT ADDRESSING, accept that the constant is added rather than subtracted. When both AUTOINCREMENT and AUTO-

DECREMENT ADDRESSING are available in a computer as a pair, one usually adds or subtracts the constant before the memory access, the other after. This is necessary for STACK or PUSH DOWN LIST operations.

AUTOINDEX ADDRESSING - Either autoincrement or autodecrement addressing.

AUXILIARY REGISTER - A register which can be treated as an extension of the accumulator. The accumulator and the auxiliary register act as a double length register in which the auxiliary can act as either the most or least significant half.

B

BACKING or BACKUP STORE - See EXTERNAL STORAGE

BACKGROUND PROCESSING - The automatic execution of lower priority computer programs when high priority programs are not using the system resources. Contrast with FOREGROUND PROCESING.

BACKSLASH - A backwards sloping slash '\'.

BASE - See RADIX.

BASE REGISTER - A register which holds a number which is added to addresses to form an absolute address. By changing the contents of the BASE REGISTER all memory addresses can be repositioned in memory without altering the individual addresses.

BASE RELATIVE ADDRESSING - A method of addressing in which the address is formed by adding the contents of the base register to the address specified in the instruction word.

BASIC - An acronym for a conversational programming language developed at Dartmouth College. 'Beginners All-Purpose Symbolic Instruction Code.' It is easy to learn and use, and is available widely on minicomputers and microcomputers..

BATCH PROCESSING - (1) Pertaining to the technique of executing a set of computer programs such that each is completed before the next program of the set is started. (2) Pertaining to the sequential input of computer programs or data. (3) Loosely, the execution of computer programs serially.

BAUD - A rate of data transmission measured in bits per second.

BENCHMARK PROBLEM - A problem used to evaluate the performance of hardware or software or both.

BINARY NUMBER SYSTEM - A number system having 2 as its base and expressing all quantities by the numerals 0 and 1. As in the decimal system, the value of binary digits is positionally weighted from right to left by ascending powers of the base.

BINARY CODED DECIMAL NOTATION - A Positional notation in which the individual decimal digits expressing a number in decimal notation are each represented by a binary numeral, e.g. the number 23 is represented by 0010 0011 in the 8-4-2-1 type of binary-coded decimal notation and by 10111 in binary notation. Abbreviated BCD.

BIPOLAR - A generic name for current controlled semiconductor devices characterised by fast operation and high power dissipation. The best known type of bipolar logic is TTL. (See TRANSISTOR TRANSISTOR LOGIC.)

BIT - A contraction of binary digit. The smallest unit of information within a character which can assume the values of 0 and 1.

BLOCK - A group of consecutive words, characters, or bits which are handled as a single unit, particularly, with respect to input/output operations.

BLOCK DIAGRAM - A chart which graphically depicts the functional relationships of hardware making up a system. The block diagram serves to indicate the various data and control paths between functional units of the system hardware.

BLOCK TRANSFER - A method of transferring data between two devices, in which the data is a set of consecutive machine words, characters, or digits handled as a unit.

BRANCH - A program instruction causing a conditional, or unconditional transfer of control to another part of the program, often referred to as a JUMP.

BREAKPOINT - A point in a computer program where normal execution is interrupted to enable visual checking, to allow debugging, or to obtain printouts.

BOOLEAN ALGEBRA - This uses an algebraic notation to express logical relationships similar to the way conventional algebra is used to express mathematical
relationships.

BOOTSTRAP - The special way of loading a program into a computer by means
of fixed preliminary instructions which in turn call in instructions to
read programs and data.

BUBBLE MEMORY - A memory using small magnetic domains or 'bubbles' as the
storage medium.

BUFFER - Either a device for isolating a signal source from its load or
a contraction of BUFFER STORE.

BUFFER STORE - A device where data is temporarily stored when information
is being transmitted from one unit to the other.

BUFFERED DEVICE - A device which is isolated from other devices with a buffer.

BULK STORE - A storage device used to store large amounts of data (e.g.
a disc.)

BUS - A major electrical path which connects two or more electrical circuits.
Sometimes known as a trunk or highway.

BUS LATCH - (See REGISTER)

BYTE - A string of 8 bits. A byte machine is a computer which works in
basic units of 8 bits.

C

CALL - A type of command which transfers program control to a specified
SUBROUTINE in such a way that control can be transferred back later to continue processing with the next instruction after the CALL.

CARD - Generally known as a punched card which contains data represented
in the form of punched holes, (normally restricted to large computers).

CAPACITY - Of a memory store. The number of bits or words or bytes that
can be stored.

CARRIAGE RETURN - A key or character causing the print position on a printer to revert to the start of the current line.

CARRIAGE RETURN/LINE FEED - Two printer functions, often performed together, which move the printing head to the left margin and roll the paper up one line.

CARRY BIT - A one-bit register which holds any overflow resulting from an arithmetic operation.

CASSETTE - A container holding magnetic tape for insertion into tape transport equipment.

CATHODE RAY TUBE (CRT) - A device used to generate pictures as found in a television or visual display.

CENTRAL PROCESSOR UNIT (CPU) - The part of a computing system which fetches, decodes and executes programmed instructions, and maintains the status of results as the program is executed. The sub-units of a CPU typically include the accumulator and operand registers, instruction decoding logic and the I/O control logic.

CHANNEL - See PORT.

CHAIN PRINTER - A high-speed printer where the type is carried past the paper by continuous chain links.

CHARACTER - One of a set of elementary symbols which may be arranged in groups to express information. The symbols may include the decimal digits 0 through 9, letters A through Z, punctuation marks and operation symbols which a computer may read, store or write.

CHARACTER EDITOR - An editor whose operation is controlled without reference to any line numbering associated with the text to be edited.

CHIP - A small piece of silicon on which an integrated circuit is fabricated. More commonly used to describe a complete encapsulated device.

CHIP-SET - A group of integrated circuits designed to function together.

CLEAR - An operation which restores a memory device or register to a prescribed state, usually zero.

CLOCK - The primary source of a synchronising signal which acts as a reference or timing frequency for the computer system.

COBOL - An acronym for Common Business-Orientated Language. COBOL is a procedural language formed by commonly used English nouns, verbs and connectives and designed specifically for application to commercial data processing problems. COBOL was developed by an American national committee of computer manufacturers and users under the auspices of the Federal Government. COBOL is characterised by ease of use and a relatively high degree of machine independence.

CODE - A system of characters and rules for representing information in a language capable of being understood and used by a computer. (See MACHINE CODE).

COMMAND FILE - A file that can be used as a source of commands to an operating system.

COMPARATOR - A device which compares two items and thereby produces a signal dependent on the result of the comparison.

COMPATIBILITY (HARDWARE) - The ability of two devices to accept and/or receive the same set of electrical signals.

COMPATIBILITY (SOFTWARE) - The ability of two computers to execute the same program.

COMPATIBILITY (UPWARDS) - The relationship between two computers in which the hardware or software of one machine is a subset of the hardware or software of the other machine.

COMPILER - A program which translates instructions written in a high level language into machine code.

COMPLEMENT (1's) - The operation which replaces each zero of a binary number with a 1 and vice-versa.

COMPLEMENT (2's) - The operation which forms the 1's complement and then adds 1. Most computers use 2's complement arithmetic, i.e. negative numbers are represented by the 2's complement of the corresponding positive number.

COMPUTER - Any device capable of accepting information, applying prescribed processes to the information, and supplying the results of these processes;

sometimes more specifically a device for performing sequences of arithmetic and logical operations; sometimes, still more specifically, a stored program digital computer capable of performing sequences of internally stored instructions, as opposed to calculators on which the sequence is impressed manually (desk calculator) or from tape or cards (card programmed calculator).

CONCATENATION - The process of merging together by placing items next to each other, and regarding them as one item, e.g. 16 concatenated with 3 gives 163.

CONDITIONAL ASSEMBLY - The assembly of selected parts of a program, when certain conditions are met.

CONDITIONAL JUMP - A departure from the sequential execution of instructions in a computer program (a jump) when given conditions are met.

CONFIGURATION - The selection and arrangement of equipment.

CONSOLE - A teletype or VDU used for communication between machine and operator.

CONSTANT - An item of numeric data used, but not altered by a program.

CONTENT(S)- The data held a location or register.

CONTROL INSTRUCTION - A machine code instruction that alters the internal status of the computer, e.g. 'enable interrupt' or 'halt'.

CONTROL UNIT - The part of the computer which directs the sequence of operations interprets the instructions, and provides the requisite signals to execute those instructions.

CONVERSATIONAL - A mode of communication between a terminal and a computer in which each entry from the terminal elicits an immediate response from the computer and vice-versa.

CORAL - A high level programming language designed for use in real time applications and developed at RRE, Malvern.

COUNTER - A device, or memory location which can be set to an initial value and incremented or decremented.

CORE MEMORY - A read-write random access memory which uses small ferrite torroids (doughnut-shaped cores) as the memory bit storage. Core memory is non-volatile: data remains in storage after removal of power.

CORE STORE - See CORE MEMORY.

CORRUPTION - A loss of data or code caused by a failure of hardware or software.

CPU - (See Central Processor Unit)

CRASH - A catastrophic program failure due to software or hardware malfunction.

CRC - Cyclic Redundancy Check. A particular type of code, appended to a block of data or program which can be used to check whether the data or program has been corrupted.

CRITICAL PATH - The sequence of inter-connected events and activities between the start of a project, and its completion that will require the longest time to accomplish. An analysis based on this gives the shortest time in which the project can be completed.

CROSS REFERENCE TABLE - A list produced after assembly, identifying references to symbols in the source program.

CROSS-SOFTWARE - Programs for the production and simulation of microprocessor software designed to run on a different machine or mini-computer.

CROWBAR - A circuit which shorts out a power supply if the supply delivers too high a voltage, thus protecting the circuits connected to it.

CRT - See Cathode Ray Tube.

CURRENT INJECTION LOGIC - See INTEGRATED INJECTION LOGIC.

CURRENT LOCATION COUNTER - A counter kept by an assembler to determine the address assigned to an instruction or constant being assembled.

CURSOR - An indication on a VDU screen showing where the next input character will be displayed.

CRYSTAL CONTROLLED CLOCK - A device that vibrates at a fixed frequency when excited electrically. It is commonly used to provide an accurate timing source for computer systems.

CYCLE STEALING - A method whereby data is transferred between an external device and memory, whilst the central processor hesitates for one (or more) cycle(s), i.e. the central processor completes the execution of an instruction and halts for one cycle during which a data word is transferred. This technique is normally used for direct memory access (qv).

CYCLE TIME - The time required by a computer to read from or write into the system memory. Cycle time is often used as a measure of computer performance, since this is a measure of the time required to fetch an instruction.

D

DAISY CHAIN - To connect each unit to it's neighbours rather than to a single point, thus forming a chain.

DATA - A collection of numeric, alphabetic or special characters denoting facts and information, in particular that which is to be processed or produced by the machine.

DATA BANK - A collection of data bases.

DATA BASE - (a) A file or collection of files designed to be shared by several users. (b) A file or collection of files which is structured to reflect inter-record relationships.

DATA LINK - A telecommunications system used for transmitting and receiving data between a computer and a remote device.

DATA PROCESSOR - A device capable of performing data processing, including desk calculators, punched card machines, and computers. Synonymous with processor.

DATA PROCESSING SYSTEM - A group of machines and people organised and acting together to process data by recording, sorting, calculating and summarising to produce a desired output. Such a system strives to minimise the need for manual handling of data and the duplication of effort. (Sometimes abbreviated to DP)

DEBUG - To isolate and remove malfunctions from a computer or mistakes from a program.

<u>DEBUGGING</u> - The process of locating and removing errors from a computer program.

<u>DECREMENT</u> - To subtract a fixed quantity or value (usually unity).

<u>DEFAULT</u> - The value which is assumed if none is specified.

<u>DEVICE</u> - A unit or processing equipment in a computer system external to the CPU; synonymous with the term peripheral.

<u>DEVICE CONTROLLER</u> - A piece of electronic equipment which organises transfer of data between a computer and a peripheral device.

<u>DEVICE INDEPENDENT</u> - A method of input/output programming in which no distinction is made betwen different types of peripheral or other devices.

<u>DIAGNOSTICS</u> - Routines designed to facilitate the location of malfunctions in computer hardware and associated peripheral equipment.

<u>DIGITAL</u> - A representation of information by digits.

<u>DIGITAL TO ANALOG(UE) CONVERTER (DAC)</u> - A device which converts digital signals into analog(ue) signals.

<u>DIGITAL COMPUTER</u> - A computer which operates on digits represented in binary form as opposed to an analogue computer which performs calculations on physical measurements, such as voltage or current.

<u>DIODE TRANSISTOR LOGIC (DTL)</u> - Electronic devices using diodes as the input elements and transistors as the inverter elements of gate circuits (qv). (No longer used).

<u>DIL</u> (Dual-in-line) - An encapsulation technique which uses two parallel rows of pins for connection to the device or more specifically a device so encapsulated.

<u>DIRECT ADDRESSING</u> - A method of addressing in which the address is contained in the machine instruction.

<u>DIRECT COUPLER</u> - A device which provides a direct data channel between two computers. It can operate via the program I/O (qv) or DMA (qv) system of either computer.

DIRECT DIGITAL CONTROL (DDC) - A method of process control in which an output from the computer (in digital form) directly controls an actuating device (e.g. valve). The computer program calculates the control actions to be taken on the actuating device. (See also SUPERVISORY CONTROL).

DIRECT MEMORY ACCESS (DMA) - A method of transferring data directly between a peripheral device and memory. Although the central processor is not used, it is usually required to hesitate for one (or more) cycles. See also CYCLE STEALING.

DIRECTORY - A record of the files on a backing store.

DISABLED INTERRUPT - A state of an interrupt system in which an interrupt request cannot be accepted by the central processor.

DISCRETE COMPONENT - A uniquely indentifiable circuit component such as a resistor, transistor, or capacitor as opposed to integrated circuits (qv).

DISK - See MAGNETIC DISK.

DISK DRIVE - A unit for reading or writing to magnetic disks.

DISPLACEMENT - See OFFSET.

DISPLAY - A visual presentation of data.

DOCUMENT - (1) A medium and the data recorded on it for human use, e.g. a report sheet, a book. (2) By extention, any record that has permanence and that can be read by man or machine.

DOCUMENTATION - (1) The creating, collecting, organising, storing, citing, and disseminating of documents or the information recorded in documents. (2) A collection of documents or information on a given subject.

DOUBLE INDIRECT ADDRESSING - A method of addressing in which the instruction references a location in memory, in which a further address is stored, (first level of indirection). The contents of this address are used to specify a further address, (second level of indirection). Finally, the contents of the last specified address are used as the operand of the memory reference instruction. See INDIRECT ADDRESSING.

DOUBLE LENGTH - Representing a data word in twice as many bits as are used in the normal computer word.

DOWN TIME - Intervals when the computer is malfunctioning, as opposed to good time, idle time, or scheduled maintenance time.

DRUM STORAGE - A storage device which uses magnetic recording on a rotating cylinder.

DUMMY - An adjective used to indicate an artificial address, record or instruction which is inserted for the sole purpose of fulfilling certain laid down conditions, as in a 'dummy variable'.

DUMP (MEMORY) - To copy the contents of all or part of memory, usually on to an external storage medium or printer for inspection.

DUPLEX (FULL) - A method of operation of a communication circuit which allows simultaneous data transmission in both directions.

DUPLEX (HALF) - A method of operation of a communication circuit which allows data transmission in one direction only at any one time.

E

EDIT - Re-arrangement, deletion or addition of data.

EDITOR - Software which permits data to be EDITED.

EFFECTIVE ADDRESS - The address actually used to reference memory. When the CPU executes a memory reference instruction (qv) it evaluates the memory address in one of several ways according to the addressing mode to form the effective address. This is then used to access the actual data required.

EMULATION - (Note difference from SIMULATION). The representation of one system by means of another functionally identical system. Thus physical phenomena can not be emulated on a computer, but the operation of another computer can be.

EMULATOR - A hardware device (sometimes incorporating software) designed as part of a particular computer, but used to execute programs originally prepared for, or intended for, a different computer.

ENABLED INTERRUPT - A state of an interrupt system in which an interrupt request can be accepted by the central processor.

END OF FILE (EOF) - A record indicating the last item of data stored in a file.

ERROR MESSAGES - A message output by a program which indicates the type of error that has occurred.

EXECUTE - To perform a specific computer instruction. To run a program.

EXECUTIVE - A routine or program designed to organise other routines or programs.

EXPRESSION - Representation of a mathematical or logical statement by symbols.

EXTENDED ADDRESSING - A method of addressing in which the effective address is formed by combining the address in the instruction (in the least significant bits of the effective address) and the contents of an extension register (in the most significant bits of the effective address). This enables a larger address to be constructed than could be achieved by using the instruction alone.

EXTENSION REGISTER - A register holding the most significant bits of memory addresses used in EXTENDED ADDRESSING.

EXTERNAL STORAGE - Storage media separate from the machine but capable of retaining information in a form acceptable to the computer, such as tapes, discs, punched cards, etc.

EXTRAPOLATION - Estimating from known values, data, etc.

F

FETCH - The action of reading data or instructions from memory.

FIELD - A set of one or more characters which represent an element of information, e.g. an address or name.

FILE - A collection of related records treated as a unit. In a computer system, a file can exist on magnetic tape, a disc, punched paper tape, punched cards, or as an accumulation of information in system memory. A file can contain data, programs or both.

FILENAME - The group of alphanumeric characters which are used to identify a file.

FILE MAINTENANCE - The activity of keeping a file up to data by adding, changing or deleting data.

FILTER - An electrical circuit designed to transmit signals in one frequency range whilst suppressing (attenuating) signals in another.

FLAG - A register or variable which is used to record the status of a device or program - in the former case it is sometimes called a 'device flag'.

FIRMWARE - A computer program that forms part of the basic computer and which is stored in read only memory. (e.g. a Loader, front panel driver or microprogram).

FIXED HEAD DISC - A type of magnetic disc drive in which a separate read/write/erase head is used for each track of the disc.

FIXED POINT - Arithmetic in which a number is specified with a constant decimal point position (c.f. floating point).

FIXED WORD LENGTH - A computer word where the number of bits in the word is constant.

FLOATING-POINT - Arithmetic in which a number is specified in two parts - a mantissa, containing the significant digits, and an exponent, denoting the power of the base by which the mantissa is to be multiplied, e.g. a decimal number 241,000,000 might be shown as 2.41,8. since it is equal to 2.41×10^8.

FLOPPY-DISC - A low cost magnetic DISC constructed of coated plastic.

FOREGROUND PROCESSING - A mode of operation in which the computer responds to commands from the external environment. It is used to described the real-time operation of a computer as opposed to the background mode of operation.

FORMAT - A predetermined arrangement of characters, fields, lines, page numbers, punctuation marks, etc.

FORTRAN - Abbreviation for FORmula TRANslator. A universal high level language especially suitable for writing programs of a mathematical nature. Developed in the USA.

FLOW CHART - A graphical representation of a sequence of operations, such as the flow of data during the execution of a program.

FOREWARD REFERENCE - A reference to a symbol that is defined in a subsequent statement, and so cannot be immediately evaluated.

G

GARBAGE - Unwanted and meaningless data recorded in input media or produced by the machine. GIGO-Garbage in- Garbage out: Jargon to express the idea that rubbish fed into the computer will produce rubbish on output.

GATE - An electronic component or circuit having several inputs and one output, designed so that the output is energised only when certain input conditions are met.

GENERAL PURPOSE - Describing a type of computer not limited by its design or method of operation to one class of applications.

GENERAL REGISTER - Once of a specified number of internal addressable registers in a CPU which can be used for temporary storage, as an accumulator, an index register, a stack pointer or for any other general purpose function.

GLOBAL - A variable, or its label, defined within a program so that it is available to one or more other programs.

GRAPHIC - A symbol produced by a process such as handwriting, drawing or printing.

H

HARD COPY - A printed output message, as opposed to a volatile display on a video terminal.

HARDWARE - The mechanical, magnetic, electronic and electrical devices or components of a computer.

HARD-WIRED - An operation or instruction which is carried out by hardware.

HEADER - A collection of data put at the start of one or more sets of data. The header will quite often contain control information etc.

HEXADECIMAL - Pertaining to the number base 16. 16 different symbols are needed to represent numbers in this system, normally the numbers 0-9 and letters A-F are used to represent hexadecimal digits.

HIGH-LEVEL LANGUAGE - A computer language which uses symbols and command statements designed to be very meaningful to an operator and hence easy to use. Each statement typically represents a series of computer instructions. Examples of high level languages are BASIC, FORTRAN, and COBOL.

HOUSEKEEPING - Pertaining to instructions, usually at the beginning of the program which are necessary but do not directly contribute to the solution of a problem (e.g. clearing fields to zero).

HYBRID COMPUTER - A combination of an analog(ue) and digital computer.

I

ILLEGAL ADDRESS - An address generated within a computer or present in a program which is outside some preset boundary.

ILLEGAL CHARACTER - A character which is not a member of the group of characters acceptable to a program or system.

IMMEDIATE ADDRESSING - A method of addressing in which the data is contained in the memory location following the instruction.

IN-CIRCUIT-EMULATION (ICE) - A facility provided on microprocessor development systems, which permits software to be debugged and monitored in the user's prototype. A probe from the development system is used to emulate the prototype's microprocessor, and simultaneously provide control over the prototype operation.

INCREMENT - To increase by a fixed amount (usually unity).

INDEXED ADDRESSING - A method of addressing in which the address is contained
in an index register, to which an offset in sometimes added.

INDEX REGISTER - A register which contains a number which may be used as
an address.

INDICATOR - A light which displays the status of the central processor or
program, usually visible on the control panel.

INDIRECT ADDRESSING - A method of addressing in which the instruction references
a location in memory where a further address is stored. The contents of
this further address are then used as the data.

INITIALISE - To set the contents of a data storage area or the condition
of peripherals to a known state before commencing processing.

IN-HOUSE - Describing facilities or expertise located within a user's own
organisation.

INPUT - To enter information into a system, or the data which is fed into
a system.

INPUT/OUTPUT (I/O) - The processes of transferring information into and
out of the computer, or the data so transferred.

INPUT/OUTPUT HANDLER - A program which organises and controls the transfer
of information between a computer and a peripheral device.

INSTRUCTION - One of the elementary operations which can be performed by
the computer.

INSTRUCTION REGISTER - A register which holds the instruction currently
being executed.

INSTRUCTION SET - The set of machine code instructions available on a particular computer. Also termed INSTRUCTION REPERTOIRE.

INTEGERS - Numbers that do not contain a fractional part.

INTEGRATED CIRCUIT (IC) - An electronic network comprising numerous active and passive circuit elements contained in a single block of semiconductor material, e.g. a silicon chip.

INTEGRATED INJECTION LOGIC - (I^2L) Merged Transistor Logic (MTL). A technology which achieves the speed of bipolar devices with the lower power consumption and circuit density of MOS.

INTELLIGENT TERMINAL - A terminal which undertakes elementary processing of input data independently of the computer to which it is connected. See also TERMINAL.

INTERACTIVE - A type of communication where each operator command is responded to individually by the computer thus forming a question and answer dialogue.

INTERFACE - The junction between two devices, e.g. the Central Processor and a peripheral device, that exchange information in a controlled manner. A standard interface facilitates the linking (by data channels and control channels) of different types of peripherals to different types of central processors. Also a device which accepts signals from one device and converts them to a form acceptable by another.

ITERATION - Repetition of a series of instructions.

INTERLEAVE - A system of input/output in which data is transferred alternately to (or from) two or more devices.

INTERLOCK - A characteristic of the operation of two or more devices, in which the operation of one device, can inhibit the operation of the others.

INTERPRETER - A program which translates and executes source language statements at run-time.

INTERRUPT - Suspension of a normal program to execute a higher priority program or service routine, as requested by a peripheral device. Afterwards, the interrupted program execution is restored at the point where it was interrupted.

INTERRUPT PROGRAM/ROUTINE - See SERVICE ROUTINE.

INTERVAL TIMER - A device which measures the time between two events, see also real time clock.

ISO - International Standards Organisation.

J

JOB - A specified group of tasks prescribed as a unit of work for a computer. A job usually includes all necessary computer programs, linkages, files and instructions to the operating system.

JUMP - (See BRANCH)

JUSTIFY - To shift a field of symbols to the left or right, to eliminate leading or trailing zeros.

K

k - Refers to 2 to the tenth power, i.e. 1024 in decimal notation. (It is also an abbreviation for the prefix kilo).

L

LABEL - A character or sequence of characters which identifies an instruction, a program, a constant, a variable or a data area. A label is the symbolic representation of an address.

LANGUAGE - A group of rules, symbols and conventions which are used to carry information.

LARGE-SCALE INTEGRATION (LSI) - High-density integrated circuits for complex logic functions. LSI circuits can range up to several thousand transistors on a one-quarter of a square inch silicon chip.

LATENCY TIME - The maximum period of time that will be encountered before a device responds.

LED - Light emitting diode.

LEVEL (INTERRUPT) - An assignment of priority in relation to other interrupts. High level interrupts are given priority over low level interrupts.

LIBRARY - A collection of standard or frequently used routines and subroutines.

LIGHT PEN - An attachment for a computer-driven cathode ray tube which transmits its position to the computer when in contact with the face of the cathode ray tube.

LINE (DISPLAYED) - A group of characters arranged horizontally which forms part of the display on a visual display unit.

LINE EDITOR - An editor whose operation is controlled primarily using line numbers associated with each line in the text to be edited.

LINE FEED - A key or character causing the print position on a printer to advance one line (without returning to the beginning of the line).

LINE PRINTER - A hard copy output device for a computer which prints on paper, strictly speaking, a line at a time, but often loosely used to refer to any printer other than a console printer.

LINK - (1) A connection between two devices. (2) A piece of wire used to modify the circuit on the printed circuit card. (3) A piece of wire which is used to connect points on a printed circuit card in order to select options (e.g. baud rates on a printer controller card).

LINKER - Software which combines the routines, subroutines, and library routines needed to form a program and produces a complete and self-contained program. The linker is often associated with the assignment of absolute addresses to instructions contained in relocatable modules.

LINKING LOADER - A program which links programs together and puts them in memory ready for execution.

<u>LIST</u> - An ordered set of items.

<u>LISTING</u> - A list of items (instructions, data etc.) printed on a peripheral device by the computer, more specifically, the visible output of an assembler showing the source program with the computer generated addresses and the machine code translations of the source program.

<u>LITERAL ADDRESSING</u> - See <u>IMMEDIATE ADDRESSING</u>.

<u>LITERAL CONSTANT</u> - A constant held in an instruction word and used by the instruction.

<u>LOAD</u> - To enter programs or data into storage or working registers.

<u>LOADER</u> - A program that causes an input device to transfer information (programs, data etc.) from that device into the computer memory.

<u>LOCATION</u> - A specific position in memory which holds an instruction or data word.

<u>LOGIC</u> - The collection of gates, registers and other components used to form a digital system.

<u>LOGIC ANALYSER</u> (Asynchronous/synchronous) - A device which repetitively monitors and stores the states of digital signals for subsequent display and analysis. The clock which inputs the information to the analyser memory can either be internal (asynchronous) or derived from the prototype under test (synchronous). Asynchronous analysers are usually used for debugging hardware with a fast clock, so that glitches can be seen, whereas synchronous analysers are more suitable for debugging software.

<u>LOGICAL</u> - A logical instruction is one normally associated with Boolean operations. A logical variable is one which may take the value 'true' or 'false' (i.e. 1 or 0).

<u>LOOP</u> - A set of instructions in which the last instruction is a jump back to the first instruction, so that the sequence can be repeated until some specified condition is satisfied.

<u>M</u>

<u>MACHINE CODE</u> - Instructions coded in binary.

<u>MACHINE LANGUAGE</u> - The lowest level programming language. A program can
only be run on a computer in machine language, thus all other types
of programs have to be 'translated' before they can be used; the translation
process is known as Assembly or Compilation.

<u>MACRO</u> - A MACRO instruction is a symbol associated with a group of instruc-
tions. When the symbol is encountered, it is replaced by the group of instructions. More particularly, an instruction in an assembly language which
is implemented in machine language by more than one machine language instruction.

<u>MAGNETIC DISC</u> - A flat circular plate with a magnetic surface on which data
can be stored by selective magnetisation of portions of the flat surface.
The information is recorded on a series of concentric tracks.

<u>MAGNETIC DRUM</u> - A circular cylinder with a magnetic surface on which data
can be stored by selective magnetisation of portions of the curved surface.

<u>MAGNETIC TAPE</u> - A tape with a magnetic surface on which data can be stored
by selective magnetisation of portions of the surface.

<u>MAIN FRAME</u> - The main part of the computer system. Typically, the main
frame refers to the Central Processor Unit. The term is also commonly used
to refer to physically large computer systems.

<u>MASK</u> - A bit pattern which selects those bits from a word of data which
are to be used in some subsequent operation.

<u>MASKABLE INTERRUPT</u> - An interrupt that can be locked-out or prevented from
occuring by the setting of a mask in the processor.

<u>MATRIX</u> - (1) In mathematics, a two-dimensional rectangular array of quan-
tities. Matrices are manipulated in accordance with the rules of matrix
algebra. (2) By extension, an array of any number of dimensions. (3)
A logic network in the form of an array of input leads and output leads
with logic elements connected at some of their intersections.

MEDIUM SCALE INTEGRATION (MSI) - A medium density integrated circuit, containing logic functions more complex than small-scale integration but less complex than large-scale integration. Most 4-bit counters, latches, and data multiplexers are considered MSI devices.

MEMORY - A general term which refers to any storage media for data. Basic memory functional types include read/write and read-only.

MEMORY CYCLE - The operations required for addressing memory and reading from, or writing to it.

MEMORY MAP - The association of memory addresses with programs, data, or physical devices using those addresses.

MEMORY PROTECT - A facility that prevents data stored in memory from being overwritten.

MEMORY REFERENCE INSTRUCTION - An instruction which refers to the contents of another memory location.

MERGED TRANSISTOR LOGIC - See INTEGRATED INJECTION LOGIC.

MICROCODE - A very low level program which controls the instruction decoding and execution logic of a computer and which defines the instruction repertoire of that computer. Microcode is not generally accessible to the user.

MICROCOMPUTER - A class of computers having all the major central processor functions contained on a single printed circuit board or single integrated circuit. A microcomputer contains a microprocessor plus additional circuitry needed to complete the system such as memory, input and output ports, and a clock generator.

MICROPROCESSOR - A realisation of the central processing part of a computer on one or more LSI circuits. Characteristics of a microprocessor include small size and low cost.

MICROPROGRAM - A program implemented in microcode.

MICROSECOND - A millionth part of a second. 1 second = 1,000,000 microseconds. The symbol (μs) is used to denote microseconds.

MILLISECOND - A thousandth part of a second. 1 second = 1,000 milliseconds. The symbol (ms) is used to denote milliseconds.

MNEMONIC - A method or artificial system of aiding or training the human memory, hence English-like abbreviations for representing machine code instructions in assembler programs.

MNEMONIC DEBUG - A debug program that interprets the machine code instructions with their associated mnemonics to help the operator.

MODEM - MOdulator-DEModulator. A device that modulates and demodulates signals transmitted over communication facilities. Used for transmitting data over telephone lines.

MODULE - An assembled printed circuit performing a distinct function, or a self contained program section.

MODULAR - A type of construction in which systems are built from independent units.

MONITOR - A program which observes, supervises, controls or verifies the operation of a computer system.

METAL OXIDE SEMICONDUCTOR (MOS) - A generic name for voltage or charge controlled semiconductor devices characterised by low power dissipation and high circuit density. N channel MOS (NMOS) and P channel MOS (PMOS) employ different types of semiconductor, and have slight differences in properties whilst retaining the characteristics of MOS.

MOVING HEAD DISC - A type of magnetic disc in which a moving read/write/erase head is used to access any of the tracks of a disc.

MPL - Microprocessor Programming Language developed by Motorola based on PL/1.

MULTI-LEVEL INDIRECT ADDRESSING - See DOUBLE INDIRECT ADDRESSING also INDIRECT ADDRESSING.

MULTIPLEXER (Sometimes Multiplexor) - A device which receives information from many independent sources and transmits the information along one channel.

MULTIPROCESSING - A processing method in which program tasks are logically and/or functionally divided among a number of independent CPUs, with the programming tasks being simultaneously executed.

MULTIPROGRAMMING - A programming technique in which two or more programs are operated on a time sharing basis, usually under control of a monitor which determines when execution of one program stops and another begins.

MULTIPLICAND - One of the factors used in multiplication. A quantity which is multiplied by another.

MULTIPLIER - A hardware unit capable of performing multiplication.

N

NANOSECOND - A thousand millionth part of a second. 1 second = 1,000,000,000 nanoseconds.

NETWORK - A structured connection of computer systems and/or peripheral devices, each remote from the others, exchanging data as necessary to peform specific tasks.

NIBBLE - A nibble is four bits, and it takes two nibbles to make a byte.

NESTING - A type of program structure in which a call to a subroutine occurs within another subroutine, or when one interrupt service routine can be interrupted by another of higher priority. Also the use of brackets within brackets in an expression.

NOISE - Extraneous signals present within a physical system.

NON-MASKABLE INTERRUPT - An interrupt that cannot be disabled by the CPU.

NORMALISE - The operation which adjusts the fractional, and correspondingly the exponent part of a floating point number (qv) until the fractional part lies within a prescribed range. In a computer, the prescribed range is generally 0.5 to 1.0 in order to obtain maximum accuracy in arithmetic operations.

O

OBJECT PROGRAM - The binary form of a source program produced by an assembler or a compiler. The object program is composed of machine-coded instructions that the computer can execute.

OCTAL - Pertaining to the number base 8, e.g. the equivalent of Octal 214 in decimal is 140, $(2 \times 8^2 + 1 \times 8 + 4 \times 1)$. The digits 0 to 7 are used, 8 and 9 being illegal.

OFF-LINE - Pertaining to the operation of input-output devices or auxiliary equipment not under direct control of the central processor.

ON-LINE - Pertaining to the operation of input-output devices under direct control of the central processor.

OFFSET - A number or constant to be added to the contents of a register to obtain the required memory address.

ON-CHIP - Functions performed within an integrated circuit.

OP-CODE - The part of a machine code instruction which indicates which function is to be performed. (Short for Operation Code.)

OPERAND - The data upon which a machine code instruction operates.

OPERATING SYSTEM - A structured set of software routines whose function is to control the execution of programs running on a computer and to supervise the input/output activities of these programs.

OPERATION CODE - See OP-CODE.

OR (EXCLUSIVE) - A logical operation between two bits which results in a 1, if one but not both of the bits is a 1, and 0 otherwise. The 'exclusive OR' operation between two binary numbers is equivalent to the 'exclusive OR' operation between the corresponding bits of the two numbers.

OR (INCLUSIVE) - A logical operation between two bits which results in a 1, if one or both of the bits is a 1, and 0 otherwise. The 'inclusive OR' operation between two binary numbers is equivalent to the 'inclusive OR' operation between the corresponding bits of the two numbers.

ORIGINAL EQUIPMENT MANUFACTURER (OEM) - A manufacturer of equipment who contracts with a computer supplier to incorporate a computer, microprocessor or ancillary equipment, within his own equipment. The complete equipment is sold by the OEM, often without reference to the supplier of the bought-in equipment concerned.

OUTPUT - To give out data from a computer, also, the data which is so given out.

OVERLAY - To replace an existing segment of a program stored in a computer memory with a segment or a series of segments retained on an external storage medium. The original segment may or may not be saved for restoration later, depending upon the program requirements. Used when the total memory requirements exceed the available main memory.

OVERVOLTAGE CROWBAR - See CROWBAR.

P

PACKAGE - A collection of items (hardware and/or software) which facilitates the implementation of a computer system in a particular range of applications.

PAGE - A continuous section of memory, corresponding to the maximum number of locations that can be specified in the address part of an instruction word, i.e. directly addressed.

PAGE REGISTER - A register which holds the number of the page which is to be referenced by the processor. It functions in the same way as an extension register.

PARAMETER - A quantity or symbol required by a macro or subroutine which cannot be specified when the routine is defined, but which is provided whenever the routine is used.

PAPER TAPE - A strip of paper used for data recording. Data is stored in the form of punched holes in the tape.

PAPER TAPE READER - A device which converts data contained on punched paper into digital signals which can be accepted by the central processor.

PARALLEL - A mode of operation in which all the bits of a word are handled simultaneously.

PARITY - A method of detecting errors in transmitted data. A transmitting device sets a specified bit (a parity bit) in the transmitted word if the word contains an odd (or even) number of bits (odd or even parity). The receiving device recomputes the parity of the incoming data and compares it with the transmitted bit. It then generates a parity error indication if they do not agree.

PASCAL - A high level language, based on ALGOL, but employing modern techniques.

PASS - A complete cycle of data input, processing and data output. A program may require to undergo several passes through an assembler or compiler in order to be translated into machine code.

PATCH - A temporary modification to a part of a program to correct an error found during program debug. A patch is usually placed in spare locations in memory and is entered by means of an unconditional branch (or jump) from the section of the program being altered.

PC BOARD - See PRINTED CIRCUIT BOARD.

PERIPHERAL EQUIPMENT - A term used to refer to card readers, magnetic tape units, printers, and other equipment bearing a similar working relation to the centre of a data processing system.

PERIPHERAL UNIT - A machine which can be attached to, but is not part of, the computer, (e.g. a line printer or disc drive).

PIN-OUT - The allocation of signals to the external connections of an integrated circuit.

PIPELINING - The process of obtaining instructions and data from memory before they are actually required, in order to speed up the operation of the machine.

PL/1 (Programming Language 1) - A language developed by IBM which is a combination of FORTRAN, COBOL and ALGOL, intended to be a universal high level language for general purposes.

PLM - A High Level language for real time application developed by INTEL based on PL/1.

PLOTTER - A device which converts data contained in electrical signals into graphical form on paper. A digital plotter receives information directly from the computer whereas an analog(ue) plotter receives data either directly in analog(ue) form or, from the computer via a digital to analog(ue) converter.

PL/Z - High Level Language developed by Zilog for real time application based on PASCAL.

POLLING - A process in which a number of peripheral devices, remote stations, or nodes in a computer network are interrogated one at a time to determine if service is required.

PORT - An input or output connection to a CPU to which peripherals can be attached.

POST-INDEXING - A method of addressing in which an indirect address is first used to access memory, and then the result is added to an index register to form the effective address.

POWER-FAIL CIRCUIT - A logic circuit that protects an operating program if primary power fails. A typical power-fail circuit informs the computer when power failure is imminent, initiating a routine that saves all volatile data. After power has been restored, the circuit initiates a routine that restores the data and restarts computer operation.

PRE-INDEXING - The method of addressing in which an indirect address is first added to the contents of an index register (qv) and the result is used as the address of the effective address. (Double indirect.)

PREPROCESSOR - A routine for converting data in a non-standard format into a format suitable for a standard utility. Also a separate computer to do such a job.

PRINTED CIRCUIT BOARD (PCB) - A board used for constructing electronic equipment in which electrical connections are produced by etching a copper coated board to leave conducting tracks where required.

PRIORITY - The sequence in which various entries and tasks are processed or peripheral devices are serviced. Priorities are based on codes associated with a task, or the positional assignment of a peripheral device within a group of devices.

PRIORITY PROCESSING - See FOREGROUND PROCESSING.

PROCESSOR - The 'heart' of the computer, where instructions are decoded and calculations performed.

PROGRAM - A series of instructions which when executed by a computer will provide the solution to a problem.

PROGRAM (TO) - To devise a program. In addition to the construction of a main program, programming may involve: analysis of the problem, preparation of a flow diagram, preparing, testing and developing subroutines, assignment of locations, specification of input and output formats, incorporation of a computer into a complete data processing system.

PROGRAMMER - (1) A person who writes programs. (2) A device for loading information in programmable read only memories (PROMS).

PROGRAM COUNTER - A register which holds the memory address of the next instruction to be obeyed by the central processor.

PROGRAM INPUT/OUTPUT - A method of input/output in which the data transfer is under the direct control of the program (contrast DMA).

PROGRAMMABLE REGISTER - A register which can be modified by the execution of a program

PROGRAMMING LANGUAGE - A language used to prepare computer programs.

PROGRAM RELATIVE ADDRESSING - A method of addressing in which the address is formed by adding the address part of the instruction word to the contents of the program counter.

PSEUDO CODE - An arbitrary code, independent of the hardware of the computer, which must be translated into computer code before being used by the computer.

PUNCHED CARD - A card recording data in the form of holes punched in specified locations. A standard punched card has 80 columns and 12 rows, each column represents a single character.

PUSH DOWN LIST - An arrangement for storing a list of items of information, so that the last item to be put in the list will be the first to be taken out again (i.e. a last-come-first-served queue). (See STACK.)

Q

QUIT - To abandon the execution of a program in a controlled manner.

R

RADIX or BASE - The number of different digits available in a numbering system (e.g. 10 in the decimal system 0-9).

RANDOM ACCESS MEMORY (RAM) - Strictly a computer memory, structured, so that the time required to access any data item stored in the memory is the same as for any other item. Now more often used to describe a semiconductor memory that can be used for reading and writing data.

READ - To pick up information from the memory, or from one of the input devices.

READ-ONLY MEMORY (ROM) - A device or medium used to store information and which may be read, but not written into, by the central processor.

RE-ENTRANT - The property of a program enabling it to be interrupted by another routine which may itself call the interrupted program without destroying the data which is needed to continue execution of the original program.

READ/WRITE MEMORY - A device or medium used to store information which may be both read or written into.

REAL-TIME - A computation or process by a computer using data derived from some external physical or mechanical process which is done fast enough to influence or control the physical or mechanical process while it is still happening.

REAL-TIME CLOCK - A timing device used by a computer to derive elapsed time between events and to control processing of time-initiated event data.

RECURSION - The process of a macro or subroutine calling itself i.e. a nested call to the same routine or macro. (Recursive routines must be re-entrant.)

REGISTER - The hardware for storing one or more computer words. Temporary storage used during the execution of instructions. May be part of, or in addition to, memory.

RELATIVE MEMORY ADDRESS - The number that specifies the difference between the ABSOLUTE ADDRESS and the BASE ADDRESS or current instruction address.

RELAY - An electromechanical device which has two stable states (open and closed) according to the state of its input, and thereby acts as an electrically controlled switch.

RELOCATABLE - Relating to programs which will work wherever loaded into memory.

REMOTE ACCESS - Pertaining to communication with a data processing facility by one or more devices that are distant from that facility.

RESET - To return register or storage locations to a specified initial condition (usually 0).

RESOLUTION (OF AN ADC AND DAC) - The number of bits into which the analog(ue) signal is digitised and vice-versa.

RESPONSE TIME - The time between the initiation of an operation and the receipt of results or an acknowledgement of receipt of the request for an operation.

ROTATE - A positional shift of bits in a register such that the bits which emerge from one end of the register are fed back into the other end.

ROUTINE - A term used to designate the whole, or more often, part of a program.

RUN - (1) The performance of a complete computer program through to its end condition. (2) Any complete automatic sequence. (3) Verb: To start a program and allow it to complete.

RUN-TIME - (1) The time required to complete a single, continuous execution of an object program. (2) Adjective: Pertaining to aspects of a program which have to be dealt with, at or immediately before running it.

S

SCAN - A mode of operation in which a group of signals is sampled consecutively. A scanner is a device which scans automatically.

SCALAR - A term used in mathematics relating to a quantity having only magnitude, not direction.

SATELLITE - A computer used in a subsidiary role to another, often performing some initial processing on input data before transmitting the data to the second computer.

SCRATCHPAD - A storage device which is used to store data temporarily. It can be independent of the computer's memory or be a specified area of memory. It is often a fast semiconductor (qv) memory.

SEMICONDUCTOR - A material whose conductivity lies between that of metals and insulators. Transistors and integrated circuits are made from semiconductors.

SERIAL - A mode of operation in which bits are handled sequentially (as opposed to parallel).

SERVICE CALL - A method of providing access to facilities within the operating system to user programs running under that system, such as disc file handling routines.

SERVICE ROUTINE - A set of instructions to perform a programmed operation, typically in response to an interrupt.

SHIFT - A positional shift of bits in a register such that the bits which emerge from the end are lost rather than put into the other end as in ROTATE.

SIMULATION - The representation of one system by means of another. In particular, the representation of physical phenomena by computers, other equipment or models, to facilitate the study of such systems or phenomena.

SMALL-SCALE INTEGRATION - The earliest form of integrated circuit technology. A typical SSI circuit contains from one to ten gates.

SOFTWARE - Programs which control the operaion of computer hardware and the associated documentation etc. needed to do so.

SOFTWARE HOUSE - An organisation providing a software preparation service under contract.

SOFTWARE PORTABILITY - The ability to run software on more than one type of computer.

SORT - A function performed by a program (usually part of a utility package) to re-arrange items in a data file into some logical order.

SOURCE - Abbreviation of SOURCE CODE.

SOURCE CODE - See SOURCE PROGRAM.

SOURCE PROGRAM - A program written in a non-machine language which must be converted to machine language by a compiler or assembler before execution.

SPOOLING - The queuing of input and output data on backing store prior to printing etc.

STACK - A sequence of storage locations. Addition of a data word to the top location of the stack causes the contents of each location in the stack to be transferred to the location immediately below (the 'push-down' operation). The contents of each location in the stack are transferred to the location immediately above whenever a data word is taken from the top location of the stack (the 'pop-off' operation). The transfer of data between locations during 'push-down' and 'pop-off' is often avoided by using a STACK

POINTER to point to the location holding the last data word added to the stack (see PUSH DOWN LIST).

STRING - A group of characters, forming a group, usually a message or other short piece of text for printing or processing.

STORE - See MEMORY.

SUBROUTINE - A short program segment which performs a specific function and is available for general use by other programs and routines.

SWAPPING - A time-sharing term referring to the transfer of a currently operating program from system memory to an external storage device, the replacement of the program by a program of higher priority, and the restoration of the temporarily stored program following execution of the high priority program.

SYMBOL - A group of characters forming a name which is associated with a memory location or numeric value.

SYMBOLIC DEBUG - A debug program which permits memory locations to be examined by reference to their symbolic names, rather than by absolute location.

SYNCHRONOUS - A mode of operation in which the rate of data transmission between two devices is related to events occurring in the rest of the system to which the devices are connected.

SYSTEM - A collection of hardware and software designed to process data for a particular application.

SYSTEM MEMORY - The part of the memory reserved for use by the operating system.

SYSTEM GENERATION - The process of preparing a complex program from its individual components, taking into account the hardware configuration of the computer system.

SYSTEMS HOUSE - An organisation providing a contract service in computer system design of both hardware and software and possibly the manufacturing of such systems.

SYSTEM CALL - See SERVICE CALL.

T

TARGET MACHINE - The microprocessor for which software is produced or which
is emulated by a system.

TERMINAL - A device by which a user can access a computer system. It will
have a means of inputting data, e.g. typewriter keyboard or paper tape reader,
and a typewriter, visual display or paper tape punch for recording the results.

TEST PROBE - A pen-like device, attached by a wire to an instrument to enable
the user to probe the electrical condition of various points on a circuit.

TEXT EDITOR - See EDITOR.

TIMER - See REAL TIME CLOCK.

TIMESHARING - A computer system in which CPU time and system resources are
shared between a number of tasks or jobs under the direction of an operating
system. The speed of the computer gives the appearance of simultaneously
performing multiple jobs. Programs performing the individual jobs are 'swapped'
at high speed under direction of the operating system.

TRACE - A routine or device which monitors the execution of a computer program
and, following the execution, prints or stores information relevant to that
instruction.

TRACE BUFFER - A memory which holds trace information.

TRACK - (1) The portion of magnetic drum, tape, or disc storage medium
which is accessible to a reading head in a given position. (2) A copper
connection between two points on a printed circuit card left after etching.

TRANSFER RATE - The rate at which bits, characters, or words, are transferred
from one device to another. It is normally quoted in kilobits per second
(kilobaud).

TRANSISTOR - TRANSISTOR LOGIC (TTL) - A technique of electronic logic device manufacture with transistors as both the input and inverter elements in the logic gates (qv).

TRANSLATE - To convert from one language or code to another.

TRANSMIT - To send data from one location and to receive the data at another location. Synonymous with transfer, move.

TRANSPORTABLE - The ability of an instruction, source language, or program to be used on more than one computer.

TURNKEY - A design and/or installation service in which the user receives a complete running system.

U

UNMASK - The operation which reverses the effect of a mask (qv) operation, i.e. it allows the central processor to accept an interrupt which was previously inhibited.

UNARY OPERATION - This is a processing operation which is carried out upon one operand, (e.g. negation).

UPDATE - To modify a file with new information according to a specified procedure.

USER MEMORY - The part of the memory reserved for use by user programs and not used by the operating system.

USER GROUP - An organisation formed of computer users to interchange information concerning a particular type (or make) of computer and its programs.

UTILITY ROUTINE - A routine available for repetitive data-handling procedures such as editing or dumping on backing store. (Alternatively UTILITY PROGRAM).

V

VARIABLE WORD LENGTH - Refers to computers in which a computer word may contain a variable number of characters. Contrasted to fixed word length.

VECTORED INTERRUPT - An interrupt causing the processor to commence execution of an interrupt program at an address determined by the interrupting device.

VERIFY - (1) To determine whether a transcription of data or other operation has been accomplished accurately. (2) To check the results of keypunching.

VIRTUAL MEMORY - Memory which appears to be available to the user but which is in fact swapped in from a backing store by the computer when required.

VISUAL DISPLAY UNIT (VDU) - An output device in the form of a cathode ray tube which can display readable information on the tube.

VOLATILE - Of a store; such that the information in the store is, or must be assumed to be, destroyed when the computer is switched off.

W

WATCHDOG TIMER - A device which causes an error indication (usually an interrupt) unless a particular machine code instruction is executed in less than a predetermined time. It provides an indication of central processor failure.

WILD CHARACTER/CARD - A character in a string which is not checked when the string is compared with another string, and which thus enables groups of similar symbols to be specified together to save typing.

WORD - A set of characters which occupies one or more storage locations and is treated by the computer as a unit and transported as such. Ordinarily a word is treated by the control unit as an instruction, and by the arithmetic unit as a quantity. Word lengths can be fixed or variable depending on the particular computer.

WORD LENGTH - A measure of the size of a word, usually specified in units such as characters or binary digits (bits).

WORKING REGISTER - A register whose contents can be modified under the control of a program.

WRITE - To record data in a storage device or data medium. The recording need not be permanent, such as the writing on a cathode ray tube display device.

WRITE PROTECT - To physically prevent write cycles to a device or memory location as a safeguard against accidental overwriting of valuable data.